THE SERIOUSLY GOOD VEGGIE STUDENT COOKBOOK

80 Easy Recipes to Make Sure You Don't Go Hungry

THE
SERIOUSLY
GOOD

80 Easy Recipes to Make Sure You Don't Go Hungry

VEGGIE
STUDENT
COOKBOOK

quadrille

CONTENTS

INTRODUCTION

Going to university is exciting. Away from the strict rules and routines of home, it's a chance to be truly independent. More than that, it's an opportunity to make more conscious decisions when it comes to the way you eat. With many more of us concerned about the environment, our health, and the rising cost of food and living, going veggie is one way to make a difference.

But, as exciting as it can be, independence isn't always easy. Between assignments, essays and exams, social plans, trying to stay at least remotely active and fitting in a few hours of sleep a night, it's hard to find the time to experiment with a new way of cooking. As a vegetarian or vegan, that often means the choice between a(nother) boring bowl of pasta, or an overpriced takeaway or ready meal. So, this cookbook aims to equip you with all the kitchen know-how you need, along with a whole load of recipes to put your new-found skills into practice. As well as being easier on your wallet (and your tastebuds!), cooking your own meals from scratch will keep your energy up, so you can actually enjoy your time at university instead of feeling sluggish.

In this cookbook, you'll find 80 seriously good veggie-friendly recipes, all based around staple ingredients like pasta, rice and potatoes that won't break the bank. Lots of them are campus-lunch or leftover-friendly, but you'll also find a few more impressive recipes for birthdays and housemate gatherings. Plus, when you go home for the holidays, you'll be armed with dishes that your family can enjoy with you – and that might convince them to go veggie, too.

Over the next few pages, you'll find our handy guide to cooking on campus, with an essential list of the kitchen equipment you really need (and what you can go without), tips for buying on a budget, a guide to what's freezer-friendly and a little bit of important info on food hygiene.

Whether you're brand new to cooking or already know your way around a kitchen, this book will teach you to make seriously good food you'll actually want to eat.

ESSENTIAL EQUIPMENT

Student kitchens can be limiting – sharing a cramped kitchen and more than likely being on a tight budget means you'll need to stick to the basics. Luckily, the following bits of kitchen kit are handy, versatile, and with a bit of care, will last you your whole time at university and beyond.

Beyond the essentials, think about what YOU like to cook and eat. If you're a keen baker, you'll want cake tins, a whisk and a wooden spoon. If you love a bean burger, don't skip the tin opener. If you're a coffee or hot chocolate addict, a good milk frother can help you save on expensive takeaway drinks – it's not quite as good, but less boring than instant coffee.

Essential
- Medium-sized non-stick frying pan
- Saucepans (1 large, 1 small)
- Oven tray
- Chopping board
- Knives (1 large, 1 small)
- Kitchen scales
- Silicone or wooden utensils
- Sieve
- Measuring jug
- Oven gloves
- Microwaveable containers

Optional
- Hand blender
- Tin (can) opener
- Wooden spoon
- Cake/muffin/loaf/brownie tins
- Glass bowl
- Measuring spoons
- Whisk

Medium-sized non-stick frying pan
With proper care, a durable, non-stick frying pan is a great choice that should last your entire time at university. Remember never to use metal utensils or cut food directly in the pan, to avoid the non-stick coating wearing off (or flaking off into your food – not very tasty or good for you!).

Saucepans
You'll want one larger saucepan for vegetables, pasta and any one-pot meals. A smaller saucepan works brilliantly for heating pasta sauces, milk or any other small quantities of food.

Oven tray
One versatile oven tray will serve you well, but if you've got some budget left over (or your parents are willing to take you to IKEA), invest in one flat pan and one deeper roasting tray.

Chopping board
This is a must – you don't want to be losing your deposit over scratches in the worktop! You can find cheap and cheerful plastic chopping boards everywhere, and they're more hygienic than wooden ones.

Knives

There's nothing more frustrating than trying to cut with blunt knives, and it's dangerous, too. Ideally, get one larger knife and one smaller.

Kitchen scales

They might not seem like an essential, but you can get a good set cheaply and they'll last you for years. Not just for baking, scales will help you portion out your meals to make meal prepping easier.

Silicone or wooden utensils

Non-metal utensils are best as you can use them with any kind of pan (see page 7).

Sieve (strainer)

This will also replace a colander, for all your carb-cooking needs.

Measuring jug

Handy for mixing anything pourable, like omelettes, eggs or pancakes.

Oven gloves

Another essential that you can find cheaply. When touching hot pans, make sure your hands and the gloves are completely dry, or they won't protect you from the heat.

Microwaveable containers

Rescuing your leftovers will help you save money and avoid food waste. Choose microwaveable, freezer-safe containers.

Hand blender

A hand blender isn't essential, but it's useful for making soups and sauces – both of which make for healthy, adaptable, budget-friendly meals. Hand blenders are cheaper than traditional blenders or food processors, but are mostly interchangeable. A handful of the recipes in this book call for one.

Tin (can) opener

Tinned (canned) food is a good, cheap way to get hold of long-lasting veggies and pulses. These days, lots of tins have ring-pull lids, so it's not an essential, but still handy to have, just in case!

Cake/muffin/loaf/brownie tins

If you know you'll want to bake in your student kitchen, you'll want cake tins, loaf tins and/or brownie tins.

Glass bowl

Again, very useful for baking, a glass bowl is handy for melting chocolate. It can also double up as a mixing bowl.

Measuring spoons

Great for rough measurements and baking.

Whisk

A whisk can be handy for cooking eggs, making sauces and for pancakes (although a fork will work in a pinch). A balloon whisk or magic whisk are both good choices.

BUYING ON A BUDGET

Buying food on a tight budget can be hard, so here are some general tips for stocking up.

TIPS FOR SHOPPING TRIPS
Make a list before you go, and actually stick to it. Whether you do a weekly trip to the grocery store or split it up into smaller shops will depend on how far the supermarkets are, and your mode of transport. You can order online, but be aware that minimum delivery charges often mean that this works out too expensive for a weekly shop.

Check prices online before you shop. If you like some widely-stocked branded products, the cheapest place to buy might change week on week. A little bit of research goes a long way!

Don't go food shopping when you're hungry. Best-case scenario, you WILL buy too much. Worst-case scenario, you will not buy anything remotely useful for the week, but will arrive home with lots of snacks.

Don't be tempted to do an uber-healthy shop with no snacks or treats. As soon as you get bored, you'll be browsing the delivery apps. Keep your food fun and eating what you've got at home won't seem like a chore.

Similarly, **have some quick options to hand.** Yes, it's healthier and cheaper to cook everything from scratch, but if you're too busy or tired on certain days, at least you won't have to resort to takeaway.

Shop in the evenings to get the best deals. When buying stickered items, remember that food needs to be cooked before its use-by date, but can be eaten within three days of being cooked, as long as you store it safely.

Work with your housemates, not against them. Club together to buy things you all often purchase. It saves on space and money. After all, you don't need four different types of oil in the cupboard!

FREEZING FOOD
Buying frozen food, and taking advantage of supermarket deals to stock up the freezer, can go a long way to helping you spend less – but you'll probably have limited freezer space, so don't be tempted to bulk buy the whole aisle! Work out what will fit and buy accordingly. Remember to portion up food before freezing (or you'll defrost the whole lot and end up throwing some away).

These foods freeze well:

• **Bread** – you probably won't get through a whole loaf before it goes bad. If you're mainly using it for toast, keep it in the freezer and chuck it straight into the toaster when you want a slice. Make sure it's sliced BEFORE freezing!

• **Vegetables and herbs** - in general, frozen veggies and herbs are great for cooking (and actually often more nutrient-dense than their fresh counterparts, since they're frozen at peak ripeness) but use fresh if you're planning to eat them raw, e.g. in salads.

• **Plant-based protein sources** - when you're tired after a long day of classes, it's so easy to throw together a pan of veggies and a protein source that can all be cooked straight from frozen. You can often get bigger packs for better value, too - a great option if you've got the freezer space!

You can safely freeze most foods, but some freeze better than others. In general, anything with a high water content is best eaten fresh, but a quick online search will tell you the best way to freeze different kinds of foods.

WHAT TO BUY FRESH

Some foods are better fresh, and it's often more convenient to have some food in the fridge that you can chuck together in between classes.

Foods with high water content like salad leaves and some fruits and vegetables are best bought and eaten fresh.

Herbs will stop your meals from becoming boring. If you plan to use them in cooking, use frozen (see left). If you want to use them fresh, swerve the plastic-wrapped packs of fresh herbs and set up a kitchen herb garden instead. You can find potted herbs relatively cheaply - and you'll save on house plants!

STOCKING UP YOUR CUPBOARDS

It's a good idea to keep your store cupboard stocked with essential items so you can always rustle up a cheap, quick, tasty meal in no time.

Have these to hand and you'll never go hungry again!

• Salt and pepper
• Sugar
• Cooking oil
• Light-tasting oil, for drizzling
• Tinned (canned) tomatoes
• Pasta
• Rice
• Potatoes
• Eggs
• Flour
• Beans
• Herbs and spices
• Stock cubes
• Condiments
• Tinned (canned) soup
• Nutritional yeast, if vegan

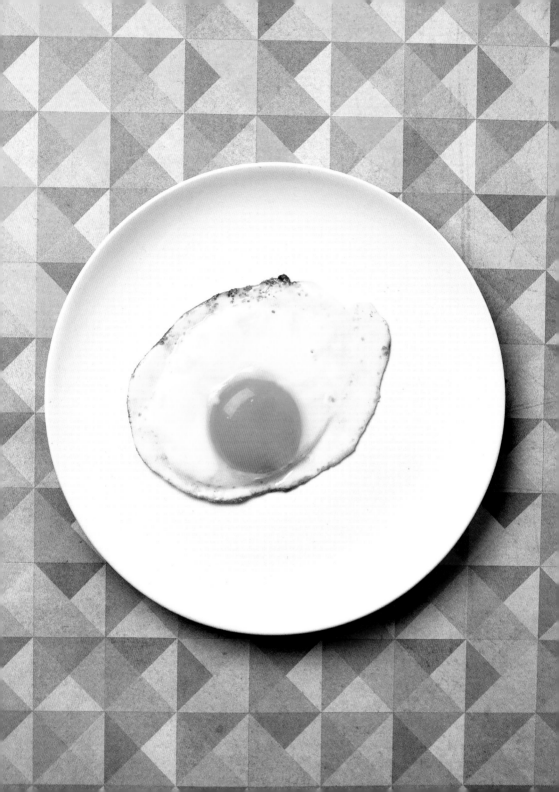

COOKING SAFELY

STORING

Read the labels! Know the difference between 'use by' and 'best before' dates. Always use food within its use-by date, and check how long you can store food once the packet has been opened. Just because it's got a use-by date of next year, it doesn't mean it'll keep indefinitely! On the other hand, if a food is 'best before' a certain date, it'll still be safe to eat a little while later – but it may have lost some of its quality and flavour. If you haven't eaten your asaparagus by the date in the packet but it looks, smells and feels fine, don't bin it. Exercise caution, and use your senses.

Inspect food before eating. Look out for signs of spoilage and throw away anything mouldy. Better yet, make use of the tips on pages 10–11 to avoid your food reaching this point.

Remember to **cool down any leftovers quickly.** Don't be fooled into thinking that you don't need to follow the same hygiene rules as meat eaters. Some of the most high-risk foods are completely veggie, like rice and potatoes.

Always **portion your meals up** before freezing to avoid wasting food.

Don't freeze food with a high water content. It's safe, but won't be very pleasant!

REHEATING

Heat until piping hot, all the way through.

Reheat food in the same way you cooked it to avoid unpleasant texture changes.

Only reheat food once, and within two days of chilling. This is especially important for higher-risk foods such as rice.

HYGIENE

You probably won't have a dishwasher, so make sure you **wash in very hot, soapy water** and replace your sponges and cloths frequently.

Always wash your greens. Surprisingly, green, leafy vegetables like spinach can carry harmful bacteria that cause foodborne illnesses, so always rinse them well under cold water – especially if you're eating them raw.

Ventilate the kitchen while cooking.

Wash out any containers immediately – especially clear plastic ones, as they tend to stain easily.

Clean as you go.

BREAKFAST
AND BRUNCH

Fluffy banana
SULTANA PANCAKES

Bananas and sultanas are a perfect combination. Leftover pancakes can be stored in the fridge for up to three days, in an airtight container. To reheat, cover with foil and place in a hot oven for 5 minutes to warm through.

 Makes:
8 pancakes

 Takes:
25 minutes

100g (¾ cup) self-raising flour
½ tsp baking powder
pinch of salt
1 tsp ground cinnamon
1 large ripe banana, mashed,
    plus sliced banana to serve
100ml (scant ½ cup) whole milk
1 large egg
1 tbsp melted butter
40g (1¼oz) sultanas
melted butter or vegetable oil,
    for frying
runny honey or maple syrup,
    to serve

In a mixing bowl, whisk together the flour, baking powder, salt and cinnamon. In a jug, stir together the mashed banana, milk, egg and melted butter. Gradually stir the wet ingredients into the dry until well combined. Don't overmix or the pancakes will be tough, though some small lumps are fine. Stir in the sultanas.

Heat a non-stick frying pan over a medium heat and brush with butter or oil. Drop 60ml (¼ cup) of batter into the pan and cook for about 1 minute, or until golden underneath. Adjust the heat as needed to ensure the pancakes don't burn underneath before they are cooked through. Flip and cook for a further 30 seconds to 1 minute. Repeat with rest of the batter. Serve straight from the pan or keep warm in a 150°C/300°F/gas 2 oven while you cook the remaining batter.

Serve the pancakes with slices of banana and a drizzle of honey or maple syrup.

Breakfast
QUESADILLA

Quesadillas are tasty and infinitely adaptable – why not chuck in your leftovers or add some veggie sausages? To turn these into freezer-friendly breakfast burritos, fill the wraps and roll up, then wrap each one in aluminium foil. Place all the wrapped burritos in one resealable freezer bag and remove and reheat as needed. Just remember to remove the foil before microwaving!

 Serves:
2–4

 **Takes:**
20 minutes

1 large ripe avocado
½ tsp ground cumin
juice of ½ lime
2 spring onions (scallions),
    finely sliced
80g (3oz) small tomatoes, such as
    cherry, chopped
3 eggs
1 tbsp soured cream or
    crème fraîche
1½ tsp harissa (optional)
knob of butter
2 tbsp finely chopped
    coriander (cilantro) leaves
4 soft white wraps
80g (3oz) grated cheddar
salt and black pepper

Halve the avocado, remove the stone and scoop out the flesh into a bowl. Use a fork to roughly mash in the cumin, lime juice and some seasoning. Fold through the spring onions and tomatoes, and set aside.

Whisk the eggs in a bowl with the soured cream, harissa, if using, and seasoning. Melt the butter in a frying pan over a medium heat. Add the eggs and gently scramble using a wooden spoon, then gently fold through the chopped coriander.

Take one wrap and spread half the avocado mixture over it evenly. Spoon over half the eggs and finish with half the grated cheddar. Top with another wrap, pressing down a little to help seal it. Repeat with the remaining ingredients.

Continues overleaf

Breakfast quesadilla
continued...

Place a dry frying pan over a medium heat. Cook one quesadilla at a time for 3 minutes, carefully flipping over with a spatula onto the other side for a further 2-3 minutes, or until the outside is crisp and the cheese is melted. Remove and fry the remaining quesadilla. Slice and serve while warm.

Coconut crêpes with
STRAWBERRY CHIA JAM

This quick-to-make jam (jelly) recipe is lower in sugar than the store-bought version. It makes more than you need but keeps well an airtight jar in the fridge for a few days. Leftover chia seeds can be added to porridge or smoothies, or combine 3 tablespoons with 1 tablespoon of water for an egg substitute.

 Makes:
10 crêpes

 Takes:
40 minutes, plus
30 minutes resting

For the jam (jelly)
500g (1lb 2oz) strawberries,
 hulled and quartered
2-3 tbsp runny honey, to taste
squeeze of lemon juice
3 tbsp chia seeds, plus extra
 if needed

For the crêpes
3 tbsp desiccated (dried shredded)
 coconut (optional)
130g (1 cup) plain (all-purpose)
 white flour
3 tbsp coconut flour
2 tbsp caster (superfine) sugar
½ tsp salt
1 large egg, lightly beaten
200ml (generous ¾ cup) coconut
 milk
1 tbsp coconut oil, melted and
 cooled, plus extra for frying
Greek-style yoghurt, to serve

Start by making the jam. Place the strawberries in a pan. Cook over a low–medium heat, stirring, until the berries release their juices, then mash them up with a wooden spoon as they begin to soften. Stir in the honey and lemon juice, increase the heat and simmer for 10 minutes, or until thickened. Remove from the heat and stir in the chia seeds. Set aside for at least 15 minutes to cool and thicken.

Meanwhile, make the crêpes. Toast the desiccated coconut in a dry frying pan, moving it about constantly with a wooden spoon, until pale gold. Transfer to a mixing bowl, then add the flours, sugar, and salt, and whisk to combine. Make a well in the centre. In a jug, whisk together the egg, coconut milk, 1 tablespoon of coconut oil and 100ml (scant ½ cup) of cold water. Gradually pour the egg mixture into the well and whisk, incorporating the flour as you go, to make a smooth batter. Don't overmix or the crêpes will be tough. Set aside to rest for at least 30 minutes, then stir in 3 tablespoons of cold water to thin it out a little.

Continues overleaf

Coconut crêpes with strawberry chia jam
continued...

Heat a non-stick frying pan over a medium-high heat and brush generously with coconut oil. Pour 60ml (¼ cup) of batter into the pan, quickly swirling the pan as you go, to cover the base. Cook for 1–2 minutes until the top starts to look dry and the bottom golden. Flip and cook for a further 30 seconds and repeat with the remaining batter.

Serve the crêpes immediately or layer them between sheets of greaseproof paper and cover loosely with a clean tea (dish) towel to keep warm. Alternatively, keep warm for a few minutes – any longer and they may dry out – in a 100°C/225°F/gas ¼ oven, layered between sheets of greaseproof paper.

To serve, spread each pancake with a tablespoon of the jam, roll up, then top with a little more jam and a splodge of yoghurt.

Sri Lankan
EGG HOPPERS

A hopper is a Sri Lankan breakfast pancake that's becoming increasingly popular in the US, the UK and beyond. Traditionally it's made using a hopper pan but a frying pan will work too.

 Makes:
about 15
hoppers

 Takes:
about 1 hour, plus
2 hours resting

½ tsp fast-action dried yeast
100ml (scant ½ cup) lukewarm
  water
250g (scant 1½ cups) rice flour
¼ tsp baking powder
pinch of bicarbonate of soda
  (baking soda)
¼ tsp caster (superfine) sugar
pinch of salt
300ml (1¼ cups) coconut milk, plus
  extra if needed
eggs, to serve

Dissolve the yeast in the lukewarm water. Sift the flour into a mixing bowl, add the baking powder, bicarbonate of soda, sugar and salt and mix well. Pour in the yeast mixture and the coconut milk, and stir to make a smooth batter. Cover and set aside to rest for 1–2 hours. Whisk well before cooking; the batter should be slightly watery and thinner than standard pancake batter, so add more coconut milk if needed.

Heat a non-stick frying pan over a medium heat until very hot. Pour a ladleful of the batter into the centre of the pan and then swirl to coat the base and sides. Crack the egg into the centre now. Cover and cook for 3–5 minutes until the hopper is golden and the egg is cooked (if using). Loosen the edges using a palette knife and gently ease out onto a plate.

Serve immediately and repeat with the remaining batter.

Mexican
ROSTADA

This 'rostada' takes Mexican-inspired flavours and layers them on a potato rösti – a bit like a hash brown – to kick-start your day in the best way possible. Sriracha sauce adds a fiery sweetness.

 Serves:
2

 **Takes:**
25 minutes

For the rostada
2 medium-sized Desiree potatoes
1 small red onion
2 tbsp plain (all-purpose) flour
½ tsp smoked paprika
½ tsp salt
2 spring onions (scallions), chopped
2 tbsp chopped coriander (cilantro)
  leaves
1 egg, lightly beaten
cooking oil
salt and black pepper

To serve
2 eggs
1 ripe avocado
juice of ½ lime
½ green chilli pepper, deseeded
  and finely sliced
soured cream (optional)
pinch of smoked paprika
a few coriander (cilantro) and mint
  leaves (optional)
sriracha or other hot sauce

Coarsely grate the potatoes and onion, wrap in a clean tea (dish) towel and squeeze out as much liquid as you can. Put them in a bowl and stir through the flour, paprika, salt, spring onions, coriander and egg. Mix well.

Heat enough oil to cover the base of your pan by about 1cm (½in) over a medium heat. Add half the rostada mixture, spooning it evenly across the pan. Fry for 3 minutes, or until golden brown, then flip over and fry the other side for a further 3 minutes until golden, crisp and cooked through. Remove the rostada with a slotted spoon and drain on paper towel Repeat with the remaining mixture.

Drain the oil from the pan and put it back over a medium heat. Crack your eggs in and fry until the white has set but the yolk remains runny, which should take about 3 minutes.

Meanwhile, peel and slice the avocado and squeeze over the lime. Top each rostada with a fried egg, the avocado, chilli, a spoonful of soured cream, if using, a sprinkling of paprika, the herbs and a drizzle of hot sauce.

Turkish
MENEMEN

This breakfast is a great one to share with housemates – why not make it for a weekend brunch? Alternatively, to save the leftovers for later, only cook as much as you'll need – say, half the sauce and two eggs – and store the leftover sauce in an airtight container. Add fresh eggs when you come to reheating. Trust us on this one!

 Serves:
2–4

 Takes:
30 minutes

2 tbsp cooking oil
1 onion, finely sliced
½ tsp cumin seeds
1 large green chilli pepper, deseeded and chopped
4 (bell) peppers of any colour, deseeded and sliced
1 x 400g (14oz) tin (can) chopped tomatoes
4 eggs
pinch of cayenne
handful of coriander (cilantro) and mint leaves, chopped (optional)
flatbreads, warmed, to serve
salt and black pepper

For the garlic yoghurt
1 large garlic clove, crushed
squeeze of lemon juice
1 tbsp light-tasting oil
140g (5oz) Greek yoghurt

Heat the oil in a large pan. Add the onion and cook slowly over a low heat for 8 minutes, until soft and golden. Stir through the cumin seeds and chilli, then cook for a further minute. Add the peppers, cook for 2–3 more minutes, then pour over the chopped tomatoes and a splash of water. Season well and allow the sauce to bubble for 5 minutes, until aromatic and slightly thickened.

Make four shallow wells in the sauce and crack in your eggs. Cook over a low heat for around 15 minutes until the whites have set but the yolks are still runny.

Meanwhile, combine the garlic, lemon and light-tasting oil with the yoghurt in a bowl and season to taste.

Sprinkle the eggs with the cayenne, seasoning and the chopped herbs. Serve directly out of the pan at the table with the garlicky yoghurt and warm flatbreads.

Green
SHAKSHUKA

Shakshuka is a tasty breakfast that takes well to whichever vegetables you have to hand. We baked the eggs in a nest of garlicky greens studded with cubes of sharp, tangy feta, but you can customize this as you like.

 Serves:
2

 Takes:
25 minutes

1 tbsp cooking oil
1 onion, finely chopped
1 garlic clove, finely chopped
½ tsp ground cumin
½ tsp ground coriander
55g (2oz) mixed shredded greens
  such as kale or chard (remove any
  thick stems)
110g (4oz) baby spinach leaves
3 tbsp double (heavy) cream
1 tbsp lemon juice
40g (1½oz) black and green
  pitted olives, roughly chopped
  (optional)
2 eggs
55g (2oz) feta
handful of chopped parsley leaves
small handful of dill sprigs
½ red chilli pepper, finely sliced
pinch of sumac (optional)
salt and freshly ground
  black pepper

Heat the oil in a small frying pan, add the onion and cook for 5 minutes over a low heat until softened. Stir through the garlic and spices, and continue to cook for a couple of minutes. Fold through the shredded greens and season well. Cover and cook for a minute, then uncover and continue to cook for a further 3 minutes. Add the baby spinach, folding through to wilt the leaves.

Stir in the cream, lemon juice and olives, if using. Make two depressions in the vegetables and crack your eggs into these. Crumble over the feta and scatter with the herbs and chilli. Season the eggs with the sumac (if using) and salt and pepper, then cook gently for 12 minutes, or until the egg whites have set. Serve in the pan at the table.

Turkish
EGGS

You won't believe how good this is until you try it. Poaching eggs is easy once you get the hang of it – but if you really need them, poaching aids are available at plenty of supermarkets.

 Serves:
2

 Takes:
10 minutes

400g (14oz) Greek yoghurt, at room temperature
zest and juice of 1 lemon, plus extra for poaching
2 garlic cloves, very finely chopped
1½ tsp tahini
4 eggs
55g (2oz) butter
¼ tsp smoked paprika
¼ tsp chilli (red pepper) flakes
a few small mint and coriander (cilantro) leaves, to serve
warmed pitta breads, to serve
salt and freshly ground black pepper

Spoon the yoghurt into a bowl and stir through the lemon zest and juice, garlic and tahini. Season with salt and pepper.

To poach your eggs, put enough water in a pan with a lid to come up to about 5cm (2in). Add a squeeze of lemon juice (this stops the whites from going stringy). Bring to the boil over a high heat – you want large bubbles to be rising to the surface. In turn, crack each egg into the water, at separate sides of the pan. Immediately turn off the heat and put the lid on. After 4–4½ minutes, depending on how runny you like your yolks, scoop out the eggs using a slotted spoon and drain on paper towel.

While the eggs are poaching, melt the butter in a small pan. Add the paprika and chilli and cook for 2 minutes, until the butter smells spicy.

Spoon the yoghurt between two bowls. Top each with two poached eggs, pour over the warm spiced butter and finish with a scattering of herbs. Serve with warm pittas for dunking.

Granola & blueberry
VEGAN PANCAKES

This is basically a selection of breakfast dishes rolled into one batch of tasty pancakes. You can use frozen blueberries – just don't be alarmed if your batter changes colour!

 Makes:
10–12 pancakes

 **Takes:**
30 minutes

For the pancakes
1 flax 'egg', made from 1 tbsp ground flax seeds (linseeds) mixed with 3 tbsp cold water, left to thicken for 10 minutes
200ml (generous ¾ cup) almond milk
1 tbsp lemon juice
1 tbsp melted coconut oil, cooled, plus extra for frying
150g (1¼ cups) plain (all-purpose) white or wholemeal flour
1 heaped tbsp caster (superfine) sugar
1 tsp baking powder
½ tsp bicarbonate of soda (baking soda)
pinch of salt
100g (3½oz) granola
100g (3½oz) blueberries, cut in half if very large

For the topping
200g (7oz) vegan Greek-style yoghurt
60g (2oz) strawberry jam (jelly) , (shop-bought, or see page 21)

Mix the ground flax seeds (linseeds) and water to make your 'egg' and leave to thicken while you do the next steps.

Combine the almond milk, lemon juice and coconut oil in a jug. In a mixing bowl, whisk together the flour, sugar, baking powder, bicarbonate of soda and salt, and make a well in the centre. Pour the flax 'egg' into the well and then gradually stir in the milk mixture, incorporating the flour as you go, to produce a thick batter. You might not need all the milk. Don't overmix; small lumps are fine.

To make the topping, stir the jam to loosen, then swirl the together with the yoghurt in a bowl until almost combined. Chill until needed.

Tip the granola into a zip-lock bag and bash with a rolling pin (or roll with a clean glass bottle) to break up any big clusters. Fold into the batter, along with the blueberries.

Heat a non-stick frying pan over a medium heat and add a little coconut oil. Pour 60ml (¼ cup) of batter into the pan to make pancakes roughly 10cm (4in) in diameter. Fry for 1–2 minutes, or until bubbling on top and golden underneath. Flip and cook for a further minute, pressing down gently with a spatula. Repeat until all the batter is used up. Serve straight from the pan, topped with the strawberry jam yoghurt.

LUNCH

Italian
FARINATA

Gram flour is made from chickpeas and can be found cheaply in the world food aisle. This dish is naturally vegan and can be eaten alone or used like a flatbread.

 Makes:
1 large
farinata

 Takes:
20 minutes, plus
30 minutes resting

125g (1 cup) chickpea (gram) flour
1 tsp salt, plus extra for sprinkling
2 tsp dried rosemary
75ml (scant ⅓ cup) light-tasting oil,
plus extra for brushing

Combine the flour, salt and rosemary in a mixing bowl, then whisk in 2 tablespoons of the oil and 250ml (1 cup) of cold water to make a smooth batter, the consistency of double (heavy) cream. Set aside to rest for 30 minutes.

Meanwhile, preheat the oven to 200°C/400°F/gas 6. Pour the remaining oil into a large, ovenproof frying pan (no plastic handles!) and place in the oven to heat up.

When the batter has rested, quickly remove the frying pan from the oven and pour the batter into the hot oil, swirling to evenly cover the base. Return to the oven and bake for about 10 minutes, until the farinata is firm and the edges are coming away from the pan. Remove from the oven and set the grill to high. Brush the top of the farinata with oil and sprinkle with more salt. Grill for 3-5 minutes until crisp and brown in patches on top. Serve warm, in slices.

Roasted vegetable
PESTO RICE

*If you want to make this salad vegan, leave out the cheese shavings at the end.
Rice pouches are convenient and add variety, if you can get them on offer.
We used a wild rice pouch but use any rice or grains that you like. You'll need
a hand blender for the dressing; if you don't have one, buy a ready-made
veggie or vegan pesto.*

 Serves:
4–6

 **Takes:**
50 minutes

1 large courgette (zucchini), sliced
   into 5mm (¼in) rounds
1 red onion, cut into wedges
1 aubergine (eggplant), cut into
   1.5cm (½in) cubes
2 (bell) peppers (red or yellow, or
   a mix), cut into chunks
2½ tbsp cooking oil
250g (1⅓ cups) rice
100g (3½oz) spinach, roughly sliced
25g (1oz) vegetarian Italian hard
   cheese shavings (optional)
salt and black pepper

For the pesto (or use ready-made)
50g (2oz) toasted almonds
50g (2oz) basil leaves
1 garlic clove, crushed
3 tbsp light-tasting oil
zest of ½ lemon and a squeeze
   of juice

Preheat the oven to 200°C/400°F/gas 6. Toss the
courgette, onion, aubergine and red and yellow
peppers in 2½ tbsp oil with some seasoning. Tip
onto parchment-lined baking trays, spreading out to
a single layer. Roast for 35-45 minutes until golden
and beginning to caramelize.

Meanwhile, cook the rice according to the packet
instructions. Drain, then spread it out on a tray and
leave to cool.

If making the pesto from scratch, blitz all the ingredients
along with 4-5 tablespoons of water using a hand
blender. Stir 5 tablespoons of the dressing through
the rice, along with the spinach. Taste and season, then
arrange on a serving plate. Spoon over the vegetables
and drizzle over the remaining dressing. Top with
shavings of hard cheese, if using, and grind over some
black pepper.

Store any leftovers in an airtight container for lunch the
next day.

Egg-in-a-hole
RAREBIT

This hearty lunch is based on a Welsh rarebit. It's a little involved, so to make it easier, leave out the egg. Most ovens – even in student rentals – have a grill (broiler); be aware that you need to keep a constant eye on what you're cooking while using it.

 Serves:
2

 Takes:
10 minutes

2 thick (2.5cm) slices country-style bread
1 egg yolk
1 tsp English mustard
70g (2½oz) finely grated mature cheddar
1 tbsp beer
1 tsp vegetarian Worcestershire sauce
dash of Tabasco
15g (½oz) butter, melted (optional)
2 whole eggs (optional)

Preheat the grill (broiler) to medium-high. To make the hole for the egg, use a 5cm (2in) round pastry cutter (or use a drinking glass, if you don't have a cutter) to stamp out a circle in the centre of each slice of bread.

To make the rarebit mixture, mix the egg yolk, mustard, cheese, beer, Worcestershire sauce and Tabasco together in a bowl. Set aside.

To cook the egg into the hole, first brush both sides of the bread with some of the melted butter. Place a non-stick frying pan over a medium heat, add the buttered bread and toast for 10 seconds. Pour a little splash of melted butter into the centre of each 'hole' and crack an egg into each. Leave for 1–2 minutes, or until the whites look as though they are about halfway set. Then carefully flip with a spatula and cook for another minute, or until the white has completely set. Transfer to a baking sheet.

Spread the rarebit mixture onto each piece of toast and place under the grill (broiler) for 1–2 minutes – you'll need to watch them like a hawk – until golden, melted and bubbling. Serve straight away.

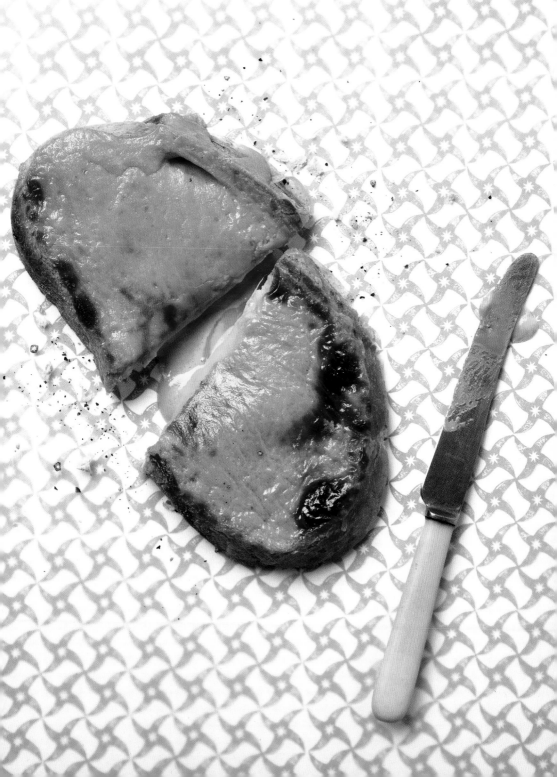

Egg mayo
OPEN SANDWICH

Egg and cress is an easy, satisfying veggie sandwich filling, and is so much more enjoyable made from scratch. Say goodbye to sad, pre-packaged sandwiches!

 Serves:
2

 **Takes:**
15 minutes

3 eggs
3 tbsp mayonnaise
¼ tsp English mustard
½ punnet of cress, leaves snipped
(optional)
2 slices bread, toasted (we used rye)
black pepper

Place the eggs in a pan, cover with cold water, bring to the boil and cook for 6 minutes. Drain and plunge the eggs into a bowl of iced water to cool, then peel and chop.

Mix the mayonnaise and mustard together in a bowl, then fold through the chopped egg, making sure it's all well coated. Stir through most of the snipped cress. Pile onto the toasted bread, scatter with the remaining cress and lots of black pepper and serve.

Cheese, egg & spinach
BUCKWHEAT GALETTES

These tasty little pancake packets make for a delicious, adaptable meal. Use regular crêpes (page 170), or mix up the fillings as you wish. You can store the cooked pancakes in the fridge for up to three days; reheat in a pan with a little butter.

Makes:
4 galettes

Takes:
1 hour 20 minutes, plus 1 hour 15 minutes resting and returning to room temperature for the batter

100g (¾ cup) buckwheat flour
½ tsp sea salt flakes
1 egg
3 tbsp whole milk
1 tbsp melted butter
melted butter or vegetable oil,
    for frying
100g (3½oz) cheddar or cheese of
    choice, grated
60g (2oz) baby spinach, chard
    or kale, very finely sliced
4 eggs

In a mixing bowl, whisk together the flour and salt, and make a well in the centre. In a jug, whisk together the egg, milk, melted butter and 180ml (scant ¾ cup) of cold water. Gradually pour the egg mixture into the well and whisk to make a smooth batter. Don't overmix. Cover with clingfilm (plastic wrap) and leave to rest in the fridge for at least 1 hour. Return the batter to room temperature before cooking. Add a splash of water, if necessary: the batter should have the consistency of single (light) cream.

Heat a non-stick frying pan over a medium heat and add butter or oil. Pour 60ml (¼ cup) of batter into the pan and quickly swirl to coat the base. Cook for 1–2 minutes until golden underneath, then flip the galette and remove the pan from the heat.

Sprinkle some cheese in a circle on top of the galette, leaving enough room in the centre to hold an egg yolk. Top the cheese with some of the spinach, then crack an egg into the centre. Return the pan to the heat and fold in the edges of the galette using a spatula to make a square. Cover – use a baking sheet if your frying pan doesn't have a lid – and cook for a few minutes until the egg white is firm and the yolk still runny.

Repeat with the remaining batter and filling ingredients.

Dosas with
POTATO CURRY

This comforting, mildly spiced potato curry is made sweet with coconut milk. Dosa mix is readily available in the world food aisle of large supermarkets.

 Serves:
2–4

 **Takes:**
1 hour 45 minutes

Instant dosa mix, prepared
   according to the packet
   instructions (optional)

For the potato curry
3 tbsp vegetable oil
1½ tsp mustard seeds
1 tsp cumin seeds
1 onion, chopped
3 small green chillies, finely sliced
pinch of salt
2 garlic cloves, finely chopped
1 tsp ground turmeric
1 heaped tsp garam masala
700g (1lb 9oz) potatoes, cut
   into 2cm (¾in) cubes
1 small tomato, chopped
½ tsp salt, plus more to taste
160ml (¾ cup) coconut milk
handful coriander (cilantro) leaves,
   chopped

Heat the oil in a frying pan over a medium-high heat until shimmering hot. Add the mustard and cumin seeds, moving them about in the oil with a wooden spoon. When the mustard seeds start to pop, reduce the heat to medium and add the onion, chillies and salt. Gently fry for about 8 minutes until soft, turning the heat down if needed to avoid burning. Stir in the garlic, turmeric and garam masala, and cook for a further 2 minutes. Add the potatoes and tomato, mixing to coat in the spiced oil. Pour in 100ml (scant ½ cup) of cold water and cook over a medium heat for 25-30 minutes, or until the potatoes are tender. You will need to add frequent splashes of water to keep the potatoes moist and prevent them sticking, but you don't want any liquid left at the end of cooking. When done, add the coconut milk and cook for a couple of minutes more. Finally, stir in the coriander.

Cook the dosas following the packet instructions, keeping them warm while you use up all the batter.

Place spoonfuls of the potato mixture in the centre of each dosa and roll into a cone shape. Serve immediately.

Mexican-inspired
SMOKY CORN SALAD

This smoky corn salad pairs beautifully with the corn & spinach fritters on page 92.

 Serves:
4

 **Takes:**
45 minutes

2 corn cobs
cooking oil, for brushing
2 large handfuls of mint leaves,
    torn (optional)
2 large handfuls of parsley leaves,
    torn
2 large handfuls of coriander
    (cilantro) leaves, torn
1 bunch spring onions (scallions),
    finely sliced
60ml (¼ cup) lime juice
90ml (⅓ cup) light-tasting oil
salt and black pepper
corn & spinach fritters (see page
    92), to serve

To make the salad, start with the corn. Heat a frying pan until very hot and brush the two corn cobs with oil. Cook for about 10 minutes, turning frequently, until tender and charred. When cool enough to handle, slice off the kernels using a sharp knife, place in a salad bowl and leave to cool.

To serve, add the remaining salad ingredients to the salad bowl and toss to coat. Serve with two fritters per person, if wanted.

Roasted garlic aïoli with
CAULIFLOWER

Charred at the edges and soft in the centre, cauliflower steaks make for a great veggie burger or sandwich filling.

 Serves:
4

 Takes:
45 minutes

1 large or 2 small cauliflowers
4 tbsp cooking oil, plus extra for
    greasing
1 tbsp smoked paprika
1 tsp ground cumin
½ tsp chilli (red pepper) flakes
salt and black pepper
3 fat garlic cloves, unpeeled
2 red onions, cut into wedges
½ lemon
4 large crusty rolls, or burger buns
    of your choice
aïoli or garlic mayonnaise
60g (2oz) rocket (arugula)
handful of shop-bought crispy
    onions

Preheat the oven to 200°C/400°F/gas 6.

Discard the cauliflower leaves and cut it horizontally into four thick steaks. Lightly grease a baking dish with oil and lay the cauli steaks on top. Mix the spices together with plenty of seasoning, then stir in 3 tablespoons of the oil. Pour over the steaks and use your hands to coat both sides. Add the garlic.

Roast for 10 minutes. Pick out the garlic, toss in the onion wedges and the remaining oil and return to the oven for 35 minutes, turning the steaks a couple of times. The steaks should be tender in the middle and golden on the outside.

Halve the rolls and chargrill, cut-side down, for a few minutes. Spread the cut sides with the aïoli. Put a handful of rocket and a cauli steak on the bottom half, followed by a spoonful of roasted onions and some crispy onions for crunch. Sandwich with the tops and serve immediately.

Halloumi & harissa
'TABBOULEH'

This Middle-Eastern dish is traditionally made with bulgar wheat, but rice is a good, cheap alternative. Pomegranate seeds are traditional and tasty but they are expensive – plan a few recipes to use them all up, or use dried fruit.

 Serves:
3

 **Takes:**
45 minutes

100g (½ cup) wholegrain rice (or whatever rice you like best)
50g (2oz) flat-leaf parsley, finely chopped
½ bunch of mint, finely chopped
4 spring onions (scallions), finely chopped
125g (4½oz) cherry tomatoes, finely chopped
100g (3½oz) cucumber, finely chopped
½ tsp allspice
juice of ½ lemon
1 tbsp light-tasting oil
250g (9oz) block of halloumi (or vegan alternative), cut into 12 slices
handful of pomegranate seeds or dried fruit such as cranberries (optional)
salt and black pepper

For the dressing
1 heaped tbsp harissa
juice of ½ lemon
2 tbsp light-tasting oil
1 tbsp honey

Cook the rice in salted water according to the packet instructions. Drain, then spread it out on a tray and leave to cool.

Combine the herbs, spring onions, tomatoes, cucumber, allspice, lemon juice, oil and some seasoning together in a bowl. Add the cooled rice and mix well. To make the dressing, mix together the harissa, lemon juice, oil, honey and seasoning.

Heat a non-stick frying pan over a medium heat and fry the halloumi slices in batches until golden brown. Top the tabbouleh with the halloumi, drizzle over the dressing and scatter with pomegranate seeds or dried fruit.

Stuffed
PEPPERS

These peppers are proper comfort food. Any leftovers are great served cold the next day.

 Serves:
6

 **Takes:**
about 1 hour
30 minutes

2 tbsp cooking oil
1 onion, finely chopped
2 large garlic cloves, crushed
150g (¾ cup) easy-cook
    long-grain rice
600ml (2½ cups) hot vegetable
    stock
6 mixed colour (bell) peppers
2 tsp allspice
250g (9oz) plant-based mince
50g (2oz) pine nuts, toasted
    (optional)
2 tbsp tomato purée (paste)
50g (2oz) raisins
1 small bunch parsley,
    finely chopped
1 tsp salt
black pepper
light-tasting oil, for drizzling

For the yoghurt
250g (9oz) Greek yoghurt or vegan
    alternative
1 garlic clove, crushed
handful of dill, finely chopped

Preheat the oven to 200°C/400°F/gas 6. Heat the oil in a frying pan and cook the onion for about 8 minutes until softened. Add the garlic and rice and stir. Turn the heat down and pour in 150ml (⅔ cup) of the stock. Cover and simmer for 10 minutes until all the liquid has been absorbed. Tip into a large bowl and leave to cool.

Slice the tops from the peppers, reserving the lids, and scoop out the seeds and core. Place in a casserole dish – trim the bottoms without making any holes to make them stand upright, if needed.

Add the allspice, mince, pine nuts, tomato purée, raisins and parsley to the cooled rice, along with 150ml (⅔ cup) of the stock, the salt and some black pepper. Spoon into the peppers, packing the mixture down. Pour over a little of the stock, then pop the pepper lids back on. Drizzle generously with oil and pour the remaining stock into the bottom of the dish. Cover with foil and bake for 45 minutes. Remove the foil and bake for a further 20 minutes.

Meanwhile, mix together the yoghurt, garlic, dill and some seasoning and serve alongside the peppers.

Smoky
SPANISH RICE

This dish can be thrown together with whatever vegetables you have to hand. We used fennel but why not try using aubergine (eggplant), courgette (zucchini) or butternut squash?

 Serves:
3–4

 **Takes:**
about 1 hour

1 large bulb fennel, cut into 2.5cm (1in) chunks

2 romano or bell peppers, thickly sliced

1 x 400g (14oz) tin (can) artichoke hearts, drained and halved

3 large garlic cloves, thickly sliced

2 tsp sweet paprika

3-4 tbsp cooking oil

25g (1oz) butter

1 large red onion, thinly sliced

200g (1 cup plus 1 tbsp) paella rice

peeled zest of ½ lemon, plus lemon wedges to serve

400ml (1¾ cups) hot vegetable stock

3 tbsp capers, drained (optional)

1 small bunch parsley, roughly chopped

salt and black pepper

Preheat the oven to 200°C/400°F/gas 6. Tip the fennel, peppers, artichokes, garlic, paprika and seasoning into a large tray lined with baking parchment. Drizzle over 2 tablespoons of the oil, toss together and spread out in a single layer. Roast for 20 minutes.

Meanwhile, heat the butter and the remaining oil in a large, lidded frying pan. Add the onion and cook for 5 minutes until softened. Tip in the rice, lemon zest and seasoning and stir for 2 minutes. Pour over the stock, bring to the boil, then turn the heat down. Cover and simmer gently for 20 minutes, or until al dente.

After the vegetables have been roasting for 20 minutes, stir through the capers, if using, and roast for a further 20 minutes.

Once the rice is al dente, increase the heat and cook for a further 5 minutes to crisp the base. Remove from the heat and set aside for 5 minutes. Top the rice with the roasted vegetables, sprinkle over the parsley and serve with lemon wedges.

Jewelled
RICE

This fragrant Persian rice is seriously impressive but extravagant, so save it for special occasions.

 Serves:
4

 **Takes:**
1 hour 20 minutes

1½ tsp ground cinnamon
10 cardamom pods, crushed
2 tsp cumin seeds, toasted
    and crushed
100g (½ cup) caster
    (superfine) sugar
2 carrots, grated
zest of 1 orange
75g (2½oz) golden raisins
50g (2oz) pistachios, toasted, plus
    extra to serve
50g (2oz) flaked (slivered) almonds,
    toasted
350g (1¾ cups) basmati rice,
    soaked in cold water for 30
    minutes
3 tbsp cooking oil
75g (2½oz) butter, plus 25g (1oz)
    melted butter
3 tbsp dried cranberries
salt and black pepper

In a small bowl, mix together the cinnamon, cardamom pods and cumin seeds, then set aside. Tip the sugar and 250ml (1 cup) of cold water into a small saucepan. Bring to the boil, reduce the liquid a little until syrupy, then stir in the carrots. Shred the orange zest, add it to the pan and simmer with the carrots for 4 minutes. Drain and mix with the raisins, pistachios and almonds.

Drain the rice and tip it into a separate saucepan. Cover with boiling water and simmer, covered, for 5 minutes, then drain and set aside.

Heat the oil and the 75g (2½oz) of butter in a large saucepan or casserole dish. Tip in one-third of the rice, then scatter over one-third of the spices, fruit and nut mixture and some seasoning. Continue layering until everything is used up. Cover the pan with a lid, then set over a medium–high heat for 4–5 minutes. Turn the heat down and cook for 15–20 minutes until the rice is cooked. Remove from the heat and set aside for 10 minutes. Spoon onto a serving platter, drizzle with the melted butter and garnish with the cranberries and roughly chopped pistachios.

Mexican
GREEN RICE

A colourful lunch that can be bulked up with the addition of eggs, cheese, beans or vegan protein sources as needed. Increase or decrease the quantity of chillies to taste.

 Serves:
4

 **Takes:**
35 minutes

100g (3½oz) spinach
1–2 jalapeño chillies, deseeded
1 large onion, quartered
1 large garlic clove
small bunch of coriander (cilantro)
small bunch of flat-leaf parsley
400ml (1¾ cups) hot vegetable
  stock
2 tbsp cooking oil
250g (1¼ cups) easy-cook
  long-grain rice
salt and black pepper
1 lime, cut into wedges, to serve

Use a hand blender to blitz the spinach, chillies, onion, garlic and most of the herbs to a paste (leave a little of each herb to serve). Add 4 tablespoons of the stock to loosen and blitz again.

Heat the oil in a large saucepan over a high heat. Add the rice and stir to coat, then fry for 2–3 minutes until starting to turn golden. Tip the paste into the pan, season well and cook, stirring for 2 minutes. Pour over the remaining stock and bring to a simmer, then turn the heat down to the lowest setting, cover and cook for 15 minutes. Turn off the heat and leave to steam for 10 minutes. Fluff with a fork and serve with the reserved herbs and lime wedges to squeeze over.

Vegan Caesar
PASTA SALAD

If you have a hand blender, why not try your hand at making your own dressing? Otherwise, there are plenty of vegetarian and vegan options available in supermarkets.

 Serves:
4

 **Takes:**
50 minutes

100g (3½oz) stale bread, cubed
½ x 400g (14oz) tin (can) chickpeas,
   drained and rinsed
3 tbsp light-tasting oil
1 tsp dried mixed herbs
2 tsp baby capers (optional)
2 garlic cloves, peeled
200g (7oz) dried pasta shells
125g (4½oz) kale leaves, shredded
salt and black pepper

For the dressing
100g (3½oz) cashew nuts
1 garlic clove, peeled
250ml (1 cup) cashew milk
2 tsp nutritional yeast, plus extra for
   sprinkling
½ tsp vegan Worcestershire sauce
a little red wine vinegar (optional)

Preheat the oven to 200°C/400°F/gas 6.

Put the cashews for the dressing in a small bowl, add cold water to cover and allow to soak for 20 minutes.

Meanwhile, place the bread cubes in a roasting tray. Pat the chickpeas dry and add to the roasting tray. Drizzle with the cooking oil, season well and sprinkle over the dried mixed herbs and capers. Crush over two of the garlic cloves and toss. Roast in the oven for 20 minutes until the croutons are golden.

While the croutons and chickpeas are roasting, cook the pasta shells in a large pan of boiling, salted water, according to the packet instructions.

Drain the cashews and blitz using a hand blender along with the remaining garlic clove, the cashew milk, nutritional yeast and vegan Worcestershire sauce. Transfer to a large bowl.

Drain the pasta and tip into the bowl of dressing. Add the kale and toss well. Season to taste, add a little vinegar for sharpness, if you think it needs it, and transfer to a platter. Scatter over the croutons, chickpeas and capers and some extra nutritional yeast, and serve.

Classic
HUMMUS

If you have a hand blender, making this classic dip from scratch will save you loads of money compared to the ready-made stuff. If you don't have a blender, try using the back of a fork to mash the ingredients for a chunkier version.

 Serves:
4

 Takes:
15 minutes

2 x 400g/14oz tins (cans) chickpeas
1 tsp ground cumin
1 tsp salt
1 small garlic clove, crushed
juice of 1 lemon
3 tbsp tahini
3 tbsp light-tasting oil

Drain the chickpeas, reserving the liquid from the tin. Blitz together all the ingredients, plus 3 tablespoons of the liquid from the chickpeas, until smooth. Resist the urge to add too much more liquid as it will make the hummus thin.

Cover and chill until required.

Pictured on page 68.

Hummus, aubergine &
BOILED EGG PITTAS

Best friends with hummus, the pitta is the perfect pocket for stuffing full of all your favourite foods.

 Serves:
4

 Takes:
20 minutes

1 quantity Classic Hummus
  (opposite)
4 eggs
2 tbsp cooking oil
1 aubergine (eggplant), chopped
  into 1.5cm (½in) cubes
salt and black pepper
4 pitta breads
handful of flat-leaf parsley leaves
cucumber spears and pickles,
  to serve (optional)

Cook the eggs in a pan of boiling water for 8 minutes, then run under cold water until completely cool. Set aside.

Heat the oil in a large frying pan over a high heat and fry the aubergine cubes for 8–10 minutes, stirring frequently, until golden and soft. Remove from the heat and season.

Quarter the eggs, toast the pitta breads and split. Fill with hummus, egg and fried aubergine and sprinkle with the parsley leaves. Serve with cucumber spears and pickles alongside, if wanted.

Pictured on page 68.

Hummus, carrot &
ZESTY GREENS

Crisp carrot and zesty greens are a great match with creamy home-made hummus. This sandwich is easy to prepare but packs a veggie punch.

 Serves:
4

 Takes:
15 minutes

½ orange
1 tbsp clear honey
2 tsp dijon mustard
2 tbsp light-tasting oil
salt and black pepper
100g (3½oz) spinach, watercress
    and rocket (arugula) salad
1 quantity Classic Hummus
    (page 66)
8 slices granary bread
1 large carrot, coarsely grated

Zest the orange and squeeze the juice into a large bowl. Add the honey, mustard and oil, and whisk until combined and emulsified. Season, then tip in the green leaves and toss to coat in the dressing.

Spread each slice of bread with hummus, scatter four slices with carrot and divide the green leaves over the top. Sandwich with the remaining slices of bread and cut into triangles before serving.

Pictured on page 68.

Hummus, tomato &
GARLIC BEANS

This is an open sandwich for garlic lovers everywhere. Simple to make but oh, so delicious.

  Serves:
4

 Takes:
30 minutes

200g (7oz) fine green beans
2 tbsp cooking oil
2 garlic cloves, finely chopped
100g (3½oz) cherry tomatoes, halved
salt and black pepper
4 large slices crusty bread
1 quantity Classic Hummus (page 66)

Cook the green beans in a large pan of boiling, salted water for 4 minutes, then run under cold water until cool. Drain and set aside.

Heat the oil in a large, non-stick frying pan over a medium-high heat. Add the garlic and sizzle for a few seconds until fragrant, then throw in the green beans and toss to coat in the garlic. Turn up the heat to high and add the tomatoes with plenty of seasoning, shaking the pan for 2–3 minutes, until the tomatoes begin to break down.

Lightly toast the bread on both sides, spread with hummus and pile with garlicky beans and tomatoes. Serve immediately.

Pictured on page 69.

Pico de gallo &
SPICY BEAN
QUESADILLAS

Quesadillas are so easy to make and versatile to boot. You can add anything into these Mexican-style sandwiches – see the breakfast variety on page 18. For best results, always add plenty of cheese.

 Serves:
4

 **Takes:**
30 minutes

For the pico de gallo
1 small onion, finely chopped
2 large tomatoes, deseeded and finely chopped
handful of coriander (cilantro), chopped
salt and black pepper

2 tbsp cooking oil, plus a drizzle
1 onion, chopped
1 garlic clove, chopped
1 red chilli, chopped
2 tsp ground cumin
1 x 400g (14oz) tin (can) borlotti beans, rinsed and drained
1 x 400g (14oz) tin (can) black beans, rinsed and drained
8 corn tortillas
150g (5½oz) mature cheddar cheese, coarsely grated

soured cream and hot sauce, to serve

Start by making the pico de gallo. Mix all the ingredients in a small bowl, season and set aside.

Heat the oil in a large, non-stick frying pan over a medium heat. Fry the onion for 5 minutes until starting to soften. Tip in the garlic, chilli and cumin and continue to fry for 2 minutes, or until fragrant. Stir in the borlotti beans and 50ml (scant ¼ cup) of water. Stir for a few minutes, breaking two-thirds of the beans up with the back of a wooden spoon – they should be mostly broken down with a few remaining whole. Fold in the black beans and heat through, then remove from the heat.

Heat a drizzle of oil in another large, non-stick frying pan over a medium heat. Add a tortilla and move around to coat in the oil. Top with one-quarter of the bean mixture and one-quarter of the cheese. Sandwich with a second tortilla, brushing a little oil on its surface. Cook for 4–5 minutes, carefully turning halfway through cooking until the tortilla is golden brown and the cheese is melting. Repeat with the remaining tortillas, beans and cheese.

Slide from the pan on to a board and cut into wedges. Serve with the pico de gallo, soured cream and hot sauce.

Indian-style
SPICY POTATOES

This sandwich is perfect any time of day or night when you are super hungry and only double carbs will do. Soft white rolls are a must if you want the ultimate comforting experience from a sandwich.

 Serves:
4

 **Takes:**
30 minutes

3 medium potatoes, peeled
2 tsp ground turmeric
75g (2½oz) softened butter
2 onions, finely sliced
2 tsp ground cumin
2 tsp mustard seeds
2 garlic cloves, finely chopped
2 green chillies, finely chopped
2.5cm (1in) piece of ginger, peeled
   and finely chopped
4 medium tomatoes, deseeded and
   finely chopped
large handful of coriander (cilantro),
   roughly chopped
salt and black pepper
8 small or 4 large soft white rolls
2 tbsp light cooking oil
1 lime, cut into wedges
mango chutney and hot sauce,
   to serve (optional)

Cut the potatoes into 2cm (¾in) cubes, then add to a pan of salted water and add half the turmeric. Bring to the boil, partially cover and cook for 8 minutes, or until tender. Drain, reserving about 1 cup of water for later. Return the potatoes to the dry pan for a few minutes to allow any excess moisture to evaporate.

Meanwhile, heat half the butter in a large frying pan over a medium heat. Add the onions, cumin and mustard seeds and cook for 5 minutes, until the onions begin to soften. Add the remaining turmeric along with the garlic, chillies and ginger and cook for 2 minutes.

Tip the potatoes into the pan with 1–2 tablespoons of the potato cooking water. Stir, breaking up the potatoes gently with the back of a spoon – you might have to add all the water to get a good texture. Gently fold through the tomatoes and most of the coriander. Season and heat through.

Split the rolls and spread with the remaining butter. Flash under a hot grill (broiler) until the butter is melted and the rolls are lightly golden. Fill each roll generously with the potato mixture and sprinkle with the reserved coriander. Serve immediately with a lime wedge, a dollop of mango chutney and hot sauce, if you like.

Fresh genovese
PESTO PASTA

This pesto will keep in the fridge in a clean jar for two weeks, or you can freeze it in an ice-cube tray, ready to add to dishes whenever you need. You can, of course, use ready-made if you don't have a hand blender.

 Makes:
1 x 350g (12oz)
jar pesto

 Takes:
10 minutes

2 garlic cloves, peeled
125g (4½oz) basil leaves
70g (2½oz) pine nuts
50ml (scant ¼ cup) light-tasting oil,
    plus extra for the jar
75g (2¾oz) vegetarian Italian hard
    cheese, freshly grated
salt and black pepper

To serve
100g (3½oz) dried pasta per person
    (we used penne)
freshly grated vegetarian Italian
    hard cheese
a few basil leaves
light-tasting oil

Blitz the garlic and a pinch of salt with a hand blender. Add the basil and pine nuts and blitz again. Scrape into a bowl and mix in the oil and cheese. Taste and add a little more oil or cheese if needed. If not using straight away, spoon into a sterilized jar and top up with light-tasting oil to cover. Place in the fridge and keep for up to two weeks.

To serve, put enough pesto into a large mixing bowl for the number of people you are serving. Add the drained penne to the bowl with a cupful of the pasta cooking water and mix together well. Spoon into serving dishes and sprinkle over a little grated hard cheese, some basil leaves and a drizzle of light-tasting oil.

Avocado & spinach
FUSILLI

Avocado makes this pasta sauce super creamy, and it's a great way of using up those ones that are just a little too soft.

 Serves:
2

 **Takes:**
25 minutes

175g (6oz) dried pasta (we used fusilli)
1 garlic cloves, peeled
100g (3½oz) spinach leaves
1 ripe avocado
light-tasting oil, for drizzling
15g (1 tbsp) roasted cashew nuts, chopped (optional)
15g (1 tbsp) roasted almonds, chopped (optional)
large handful of coriander (cilantro), chopped
1 lime
25g (1oz) feta (optional)
salt and black pepper

Cook the fusilli in a large pan of boiling, salted water, according to the packet instructions. When cooked, drain the pasta, reserving a cupful of the pasta water for later, and tip back into the pan.

While the pasta is cooking, use a hand blender to briefly blitz the garlic, spinach and the flesh from the avocado, along with a little oil and some seasoning. Add a splash of the reserved pasta cooking water and blitz again until smooth.

If using, put the chopped cashew nuts, almonds and coriander in a bowl. Squeeze over the juice of ½ lime, season and drizzle with oil. Cut the other half of the lime into wedges.

Add a few splashes of pasta water to your pan of cooked pasta, then pour over the sauce. Toss together, seasoning to taste. Portion on to plates, spoon over the nut dressing, crumble over the feta, if using, and serve with the lime wedges.

Garlic & tahini with
FALAFEL

Making falafels from scratch requires a little effort and a hand blender, but the result is so rewarding. These go really well with the Classic Hummus on page 66.

 Serves:
4

 Takes:
1 hour

For the garlic tahini sauce
6 tbsp natural yoghurt
4 tbsp mayonnaise
juice of 1 lemon
1 large garlic clove, crushed
4 tbsp tahini

For the falafel (or use shop-bought)
1 x 400g (14oz) tin (can) chickpeas
½ tsp bicarbonate of soda (baking soda)
3 garlic cloves, roughly chopped
1 onion, roughly chopped
1 mild red chilli, roughly chopped
1 tbsp ground cumin
1 tbsp ground coriander
1 tsp sumac, plus extra to serve
handful of parsley, chopped
5 tbsp plain (all-purpose) flour
salt and black pepper
150ml (⅔ cup) light-tasting oil

4 fluffy white flatbreads
crisp chopped salad
pickled veg such as chillies and turnips, to serve

To make the garlic tahini sauce, mix all the ingredients together, cover and chill.

Drain the chickpeas and dry thoroughly on paper towel. Roughly chop, then add the bicarbonate of soda. Add the garlic, onion, chilli, spices and parsley, then blitz using a hand blender until you have a coarse purée. Add the flour, season and mix well. Divide the mixture into 20 equal portions. Using damp hands, shape the mixture into little patties and place on to a baking sheet. Chill for 10 minutes.

Heat a large, non-stick frying pan over a medium heat. Add about one-third of the oil, then cook the falafels in batches for 6–7 minutes, turning halfway through, until golden and crisp. Drain on paper towel, then transfer to a warm oven while you fry the remaining falafels in the rest of the oil.

Serve five falafels per person on a flatbread, spoon over some of the garlic tahini sauce and serve with some chopped salad and pickles, if using.

Courgette & broccoli
PASTA SALAD

An easy pasta salad dish that travels well, and is super fresh and light for summer lunches.

 Serves:
2

 Takes:
30 minutes

100g (3½oz) dried pasta (we used orecchiette)
20g (⅔oz) basil, leaves picked
½ garlic clove, peeled
3 tbsp light-tasting oil
1 courgette (zucchini)
100g (3½oz) tenderstem broccoli (broccolini), trimmed into florets
5g (1 tsp) vegetarian Italian hard cheese, freshly grated
15g (2 tbsp) toasted flaked (slivered) almonds (optional)
salt and black pepper

Cook the orecchiette in a pan of boiling, salted water, according to the packet instructions. Drain into a colander and run under the cold tap until just warm.

While the pasta is cooking, use a hand blender to blitz the basil leaves, garlic and a pinch of salt to a paste. Add the light-tasting oil.

Place a frying pan on a high heat. Use a swivel peeler to peel long strips of courgette, then fry the courgette and broccoli in batches. Transfer to the bowl of dressing. Tip the warm, drained pasta into the bowl of dressed vegetables. Toss with the grated hard cheese, then divide between dishes, scatter over the almonds and serve.

Cauliflower & broccoli
CHEESY BAKE

Rich, madly cheesy and the perfect bake on a cold day. Serve on its own with lots of black pepper, and maybe a salad.

 Serves:
4–6

 Takes:
1 hour

cooking oil, for greasing
900ml (3¾ cups) milk
50g (2oz) unsalted butter
3 tbsp plain (all-purpose) flour
2 tsp English mustard
100g (3½oz) mature cheddar, grated
50g (2oz) vegetarian blue cheese, grated, if liked (or use more of the other cheeses)
50g (2oz) vegetarian Italian hard cheese, finely grated
200g (7oz) dried pasta (we used farfalle)
300g (10oz) mixture of cauliflower and broccoli florets, cut into small pieces
salt and black pepper

Preheat the oven to 220°C/425°F/gas 7. Oil a 30x20cm (12x8in) baking dish.

Put the milk in a saucepan, place on a low heat, bring to a simmer, then take off the heat.

Melt the butter in a medium saucepan on a low heat, then stir in the flour and mustard for a minute. A ladleful at a time, add the warm milk to the pan, stirring for about 5–10 minutes, until the sauce has thickened and coats the back of a spoon. Stir in most of each of the cheeses, season to taste and take off the heat.

Cook the farfalle in a large pan of boiling, salted water for half the cooking time stated on the packet, adding the cauliflower and broccoli for the final 3 minutes, then drain.

Tip the pasta and vegetables into the sauce, stir together and spoon into the oiled baking dish. Scatter with the remaining cheeses and a grind of pepper, then bake for 20 minutes until golden and bubbling.

LIGHT BITES

Egg-fried
RICE CAKES

These mini egg-fried rice cakes are perfect for a snack, but the rice can also be a meal in its own right, especially if you throw in a few extra ingredients. This is fantastic for using up any leftovers.

Makes:
12

Takes:
30 minutes, plus soaking, cooling and chilling

100g (3½oz) risotto rice
1 tbsp cooking oil
4 spring onions (scallions), finely sliced
1 fat garlic clove, finely chopped
¼ tsp chilli (red pepper) flakes
80g (3oz) frozen shelled edamame, defrosted (optional)
3 eggs, beaten
1 tbsp soy sauce
handful of coriander (cilantro) leaves, finely chopped
4 tbsp panko breadcrumbs
cooking oil
sweet chilli sauce, to serve

Place the rice in a pan with 200ml (generous ¾ cup) of salted water. Bring to the boil, then cover and simmer gently for 10 minutes. Remove from the heat and leave, covered, for 10 minutes, or until the water is absorbed and the rice tender.

Heat the oil in a large frying pan. Add the spring onions, garlic and chilli flakes. Stir fry over a high heat for 1 minute. Add the edamame and the cooked rice and pour in the whisked eggs. When the bottom starts to set, use a wooden spoon to scramble the eggs. Remove from the heat, add the soy sauce and fork through the rice. Spread the rice over a large plate, press cling film (plastic wrap) onto the surface and leave to cool for 10 minutes.

Transfer the rice to a bowl and mix through the coriander. Using wet hands, divide the rice into 12 small cakes. Press the top and bottom lightly into some breadcrumbs, then chill for 15 minutes. Heat enough oil in a large frying pan to come about 1cm (½in) up the sides. Fry the cakes in batches for 2-3 minutes on each side, until golden, crisp and piping hot throughout. Serve with sweet chilli sauce for dipping.

Baked
EGGS IN POTATOES

These are best eaten warm, so prepare them in advance and, when ready to serve, crack in your eggs and pop them in the oven.

 Makes:
4

 Takes:
1 hr 30 mins–2 hrs,
plus cooling

2 baking potatoes
drizzle of cooking oil
30g (1oz) finely grated cheddar
2 tsp soured cream, plus extra
   to serve
a few snipped chives (optional)
1 spring onion (scallion), trimmed
   and finely chopped
4 small eggs
salt and black pepper

Preheat the oven to 220°C/425°F/gas 7. Place the potatoes on a baking tray, drizzle with oil and season with salt and pepper, and roll around to coat. Prick the skin, then bake for 1–1½ hours, until crisp and golden. Remove and set aside until cool enough to handle. Cut each potato in half lengthways and with a small teaspoon, scoop out the flesh into a bowl, leaving a good amount around the edges to support the skins.

Mash the potato flesh a little with a fork to get rid of any large lumps, then fold through the grated cheese, soured cream, chives and spring onion. Season with salt and pepper.

Scoop the potato mixture back into the skins, make a well in the middle of each one (in which you'll bake the eggs) and place on a baking tray. Crack each egg in turn, letting a little of the white drain into a bowl, before filling the potato skins. Season with a little salt and pepper.

Bake in the oven for 8–10 minutes, or until the egg whites have set. Remove and serve while warm, with soured cream for dipping.

Tomato salsa with
CORN & SPINACH FRITTERS

Sweet and juicy corn kernels really make these pancakes pop with flavour.
Kernels cut fresh from the cob are ideal, but the canned stuff also works nicely.

 Makes:
8 fritters

 Takes:
30 minutes

For the salsa
3 ripe tomatoes, about 160g (5½oz), finely chopped
1 red onion, finely sliced
60g (2oz) feta, crumbled
1 tbsp lime juice, or more to taste
3 tbsp light-tasting oil
salt
black pepper

For the fritters
160g (1¼ cups) self-raising flour
1 tsp salt
1 tsp ground coriander
½ tsp ground cumin
1 tsp smoked paprika
1 egg, lightly beaten
1 tbsp cooking oil, plus extra for frying
250g (9oz) corn kernels, from corn cobs or a tin (can)
60g (2oz) spinach, finely sliced

Make the salsa by combining all the ingredients in a bowl. Set aside to allow the flavours to mingle.

For the fritters, whisk together the flour, salt and spices. Stir in the egg and oil, and then 130ml (½ cup) of cold water, or enough to make a smooth batter. Fold in the corn and spinach – the batter will be very thick.

Heat a frying pan over a high heat and brush with oil. Reduce the heat to medium and pour 60ml (¼ cup) of batter into the pan. Use the back of a spoon to flatten the batter into a patty shape and cook for 2 minutes on each side, until golden and cooked through. Repeat with the remaining batter.

Serve the fritters hot, with a big spoonful of salsa on the side. They are also delicious served with a fried egg on top.

Gallo
PINTO

This is eaten morning, noon and night all over Costa Rica and Nicaragua, but both countries dispute the origin of this simple meal of rice and beans. The name translates as 'spotted rooster' in Spanish and refers to the speckled appearance of the dish.

 Serves:
4

 Takes:
25 minutes

175g (1 cup) long-grain rice
2 tbsp coconut or cooking oil
1 onion, finely chopped
1 red (bell) pepper, finely chopped
2 garlic cloves, finely chopped
1 tsp ground cumin
1 tsp ground coriander
1 x 400g (14oz) tin (can) black
    beans, rinsed and drained
2 tsp vegan Worcestershire sauce
few shakes of Tabasco
small bunch of coriander (cilantro)
    leaves, finely chopped
salt and black pepper

Cook the rice in salted water according to the packet instructions.

Heat the oil in a saucepan and fry the onion and red pepper for 10 minutes. Add the garlic and spices and stir, then turn up the heat a little and tip in the beans. Cook for 4–5 minutes, stirring, until they begin to crisp, then stir in the cooked rice. Add 5–6 tablespoons of cold water to the pan and warm through. Splash in the Worcestershire sauce and Tabasco. Season and stir through the coriander.

Courgette &
HALLOUMI FRITTERS

These fritters are bursting with spring flavours. Enjoy them with a hefty dose of sunshine if you can. If you don't have buttermilk, combine the same amount of milk with 1 tablespoon of lemon juice and leave to rest for 15 minutes before using.

 Makes:
12 fritters

 **Takes:**
25 minutes

150g (1¼ cups) plain (all-purpose) flour
1 tsp baking powder
½ tsp bicarbonate of soda (baking soda)
½ tsp sea salt
1 heaped tbsp caster (superfine) sugar
250ml (1 cup) buttermilk (or see above)
1 large egg, lightly beaten
1 tbsp melted butter
2 medium courgettes (zucchini)
1 tsp salt
200g (7oz) halloumi, grated
handful of basil leaves, torn (optional)
handful of mint leaves, finely sliced (optional)
3 spring onions (scallions), finely sliced
grated zest of 1 lemon
black pepper
cooking oil
pea shoots and lemon wedges, to serve (optional but recommended)

In a mixing bowl, whisk together the flour, baking powder, bicarbonate of soda, salt and sugar, and make a well in the centre. In a jug, whisk together the buttermilk, egg and melted butter. Gradually pour the egg mixture into the well and whisk, incorporating the flour as you go, to make a smooth batter. Don't overmix or the fritters will be tough. Some small lumps are fine.

Grate the courgettes on the largest holes of a box grater. Transfer to a sieve set over a bowl and toss with the salt. Set aside for 15 minutes to drain, then place in a clean tea (dish) towel and squeeze tightly to remove as much liquid as possible. Loosen the courgettes – they'll be tightly packed together – then add to the pancake batter along with all the remaining ingredients except the oil, pea shoots and lemon wedges.

Heat a non-stick frying pan over a medium heat and brush generously with the oil. Add large spoonfuls of batter to the pan to make 10cm (4in) pancakes and cook for 2 minutes until golden underneath. Flip and cook for a further 2 minutes.

Serve the pancakes sprinkled with salt and a handful of pea shoots with lemon wedges on the side.

Squash, courgette &
MINTY FETA

Roasting the squash with fragrant spices heightens its natural sweetness. You could also use this to fill a courgette. To minimize prep time, use pre-cut butternut squash slices. Make sure you get fresh mint for the feta.

 Serves:
4

 Takes:
I hour

1 butternut squash
2 tbsp cooking oil, plus a glug
4 garlic cloves, unpeeled
1 tsp chilli (red pepper) flakes
1 tsp ground cinnamon
1 tsp sweet smoked paprika
salt and black pepper
2 courgettes (zucchinis), cut into
   5mm slices lengthways
200g (7oz) feta cheese
100g (3½oz) thick Greek yoghurt
handful of mint, finely chopped
8 slices crusty granary bread
handful of pitted Kalamata
   olives, roughly chopped
   (optional)

Preheat the oven to 190°C/375°F/gas 5.

Peel the squash, halve lengthways (you'll need a very sharp knife for this – watch your fingers!), scoop out the seeds and cut into 1cm (⅜in) thick slices, then tip into a roasting tray and toss with the oil, garlic, chilli, cinnamon, paprika and seasoning. Roast for 45 minutes, picking out and reserving the garlic halfway through cooking. Gently stir the squash and continue to cook until soft and caramelized.

Meanwhile, heat a griddle pan or frying pan over a high heat. Brush the courgettes with a little oil, then cook for 3-5 minutes, turning halfway through, or until charred and starting to soften. Remove and set aside.

Squeeze the garlic cloves out of their skins, add to a bowl and mash with a fork. Crumble in the feta and yoghurt. Stir to combine, season, then add most of the mint. Set aside.

To assemble the sandwiches, spread the bread with equal amounts of the feta mixture. Divide the courgette and squash between four slices and dot over the olives (if using) and the reserved mint. Sandwich with the remaining four slices and serve.

Pudla with
COCONUT CHUTNEY

These are delicious and also good for you, containing nothing more than chickpeas, vegetables, garlic and herbs. Homemade chutney is delicious but if you don't own a hand blender, shop-bought will work nicely too.

 Makes:
8 pudla

 **Takes:**
45 minutes

For the pudla
150g (1½ cups) gram flour
3 tbsp chopped coriander (cilantro)
1 green chilli, finely chopped
1 tsp cumin (seeds or ground)
1 tsp salt
1 tsp cooking oil, plus extra
large handful of grated vegetables
    e.g. carrots, courgettes (zucchinis)
    or spring onions (scallions)

For the chutney
80g (3oz) desiccated (dried
    shredded) coconut
2 large handfuls of coriander
    (cilantro) leaves and thin stalks
2 large handfuls of mint leaves
8 medium green chillies
8 garlic cloves
2 tsp cumin seeds
120ml (½ cup) coconut
    milk, plus extra if needed
2 tsp caster (superfine) sugar
60ml (¼ cup) lime juice,
    plus more to taste
salt

Start by making the pudla. In a mixing bowl, whisk together the chickpea flour, coriander, chilli, cumin and salt. Gradually stir in the oil along with about 250ml (1 cup) of cold water to make a batter the consistency of single (light) cream. Set aside to rest for 1 hour.

Meanwhile, if making the chutney from scratch, soak the coconut in 150ml (generous ½ cup) cold water for 30 minutes, then drain and squeeze out the excess liquid. Using a hand blender, blitz the soaked coconut with the remaining chutney ingredients until well combined and creamy, but still with some texture. Taste and add more lime juice or salt if needed, or more coconut milk if the chutney is too thick. Transfer to a bowl and set aside.

Stir the vegetables into the pudla batter. Heat a frying pan over a high heat and brush generously with oil. Pour 60ml (¼ cup) of batter into the pan, swirling to coat the base. Reduce the heat to medium–high and cook for 3-4 minutes until bubbles start to form and the top begins to look dry. Loosen the edges with a spatula, flip and cook for 1-2 minutes. Transfer to a plate, cover loosely with foil and repeat with the remaining batter.

Serve the pudla hot with the chutney alongside for dunking, or wrapped inside, if you prefer.

Cheesy
RICE FRITTERS

These cheesy fritters are great for using up leftover rice. Jazz them up by adding whatever herbs or veggies you fancy. They're great plain with mango chutney or a dollop of ketchup, too.

 Makes:
12–16 fritters

 **Takes:**
50 minutes

150g (¾ cup) easy-cook long-grain rice (white or wholegrain)
1 onion, coarsely grated
100g (3½oz) mature cheddar, grated
50g (generous ⅓ cup) plain (all-purpose) flour
¼ whole nutmeg, freshly grated
2 eggs
2 tsp dijon mustard
5 tbsp milk
2-3 tbsp cooking oil
salt and black pepper
tomato ketchup, sweet tomato and chilli relish or mango chutney, to serve

Cook the rice in salted water according to the packet instructions. Drain, then spread it out on a tray and leave to cool.

Tip the rice into a large bowl and add the onion, cheddar, flour, nutmeg and plenty of seasoning. In a separate bowl beat together the eggs, mustard and milk, then pour over the rice and stir to combine.

Heat 1 tablespoon of the oil in a large, non-stick frying pan over a medium–high heat. Spoon heaped tablespoons of the mixture into the pan and spread out a little using the back of the spoon. Fry for about 3 minutes on each side until golden brown, then transfer to a plate lined with paper towel. Add a little more oil to the pan and continue with the remaining batter. Serve with your choice of sauce or chutney.

Lemon
RICE

Chana dhal are lentils available from the world food aisle in most supermarkets. If you can't find them, use whichever lentils you have to hand. Make sure you soak them properly and fry them until really golden or they'll be on the crunchy side.

 Serves:
4–6

 Takes:
40 minutes

75g (2½oz) chana dhal
250g (1¼ cups) basmati rice
3 tbsp cooking oil
1 tbsp black mustard seeds
50g (2oz) cashew nuts (optional)
12 fresh curry leaves (simply leave
   out if you can't find any)
2 green chillies, finely chopped
4cm (1½in) piece of ginger, peeled
   and finely chopped
1 tsp turmeric
1 tsp onion powder
zest and juice of 1½ lemons
salt

Soak the chana dhal in boiling water for 30 minutes, then drain. Cook the rice in salted water according to the packet instructions.

Heat the oil in a large frying pan over a high heat. Add the mustard seeds and fry until beginning to pop. Then add the chana dhal and fry for 4 minutes until golden brown. Throw in the cashews, curry leaves (if using), chillies and ginger and fry for 1-2 minutes until golden. Add the turmeric and onion powder and stir for 30 seconds. Stir through the rice until well coated and hot, then remove from the heat. Mix in the lemon zest and juice, along with a little salt.

Green goddess sauce with
HALLOUMI

As soon as you taste this, you'll see why it's called green goddess sauce – it's heavenly. A griddle pan will create those lovely char marks, but if you don't have one, a frying pan will do!

 Serves:
4

 Takes:
20 minutes

For the green goddess sauce
1 ripe avocado, stoned and peeled
juice of ½ lemon
2 tbsp Greek yoghurt
1 mild green chilli, roughly chopped
½ garlic clove, crushed
handful of coriander (cilantro)
salt and black pepper

250g (9oz) block halloumi cheese
8 small tomatoes (we used baby plum)
light-tasting oil
8 slices sourdough bread

Start by making the green goddess sauce. Roughly chop the avocado. Using a hand blender, blitz with the lemon juice, yogurt, chilli and garlic. Roughly chop most of the coriander and add it to the other ingredients, reserving a few leaves. Season and blitz until almost smooth. Cover and set aside.

Heat a griddle pan (or frying pan) over a high heat. Cut the halloumi into eight slices and cook for 5 minutes, turning halfway through until charred and soft. Add the tomatoes to the pan. Griddle the tomatoes for 2-3 minutes – you just want them to begin to soften and the skins to pop. Remove, halve the tomatoes and season with a little salt and a drizzle of oil.

Griddle the bread on both sides until warm and lightly toasted. Spread four slices with green goddess sauce, then lay a couple of slices of halloumi and some tomato halves on top. Finish with a sprinkle of the reserved coriander leaves and sandwich with the remaining bread.

Curried
RICE

This colourful rice dish is an easy light lunch to enjoy on campus. You can alternate with whatever nuts and dried fruit you have to hand.

 Serves:
4

 Takes:
30 minutes

200g (1 cup) plus 2 tbsp
   basmati rice
1 bunch of parsley
1 green (bell) pepper, deseeded
   and finely chopped
1 small red onion, finely chopped
50g (2oz) dried apricots, sliced
50g (2oz) raisins
25g (1oz) flaked (slivered)
   almonds, toasted
salt and black pepper

For the dressing
4 tbsp light-tasting oil
1 tbsp white wine vinegar
1 garlic clove, crushed
1 tbsp lemon juice
¼ tsp sugar
1 tsp curry powder

Cook the rice in salted water according to the packet instructions. Drain, then spread it out on a tray and leave to cool. Meanwhile, mix together the dressing ingredients in a small bowl and season well.

Transfer the rice to a large bowl. Finely chop half the parsley and add to the bowl along with the green pepper, onion, apricots and raisins. Tear over the remaining parsley, reserving some for garnish, pour over the dressing and mix everything together. Scatter with the almonds and remaining parsley before serving.

DINNER

Lemon pasta with a
GARLIC CRUMB

Pasta doesn't need a lot added to it to feel special. This is best made fresh so if you're not sharing with housemates, halve the recipe.

Serves:
2

Takes:
50 minutes,
plus chilling

2 tbsp cooking oil
75g (2¾oz) breadcrumbs
1 tsp garlic granules
1 tsp dried parsley
100g (3½oz) unsalted butter
grated zest and juice of 1 lemon
150ml (⅔ cup) double (heavy)
    cream
50g (2oz) vegetarian Italian hard
    cheese, freshly grated
salt and black pepper
100g (3½oz) dried pasta per person
    (we used tagliatelle)

Heat the oil in a frying pan on a medium heat, tip in the breadcrumbs, garlic and parsley and sauté for 5-10 minutes until golden. Spoon into a bowl lined with paper towel.

Bring a large pan of salted water to the boil. Meanwhile, melt the butter in a small saucepan and add a good pinch each of salt and pepper, followed by the lemon zest and juice. Stir in the cream and most of the hard cheese.

Boil the pasta according to the packet instructions. Drain, reserving a cupful of the cooking water, and return the pasta to the pan. Tip the sauce into the pan and toss, adding a little pasta water if needed. Serve with the crumb and remaining cheese sprinkled over.

Florentine
PIZZA

*This makes enough for two pizzas – get your housemates involved, or
simply halve the recipe. This recipe is as fancy or as basic as you like
– upgrade your bases and toppings as you wish.*

 Serves:
2–4

 **Takes:**
40 minutes, plus rising

2 x shop-bought pizza bases (we
used sourdough)

For the pizza topping
160g (6oz) tomato passata,
seasoned with dried oregano, salt
and pepper
125g (4½oz) mozzarella, torn
150g (5½oz) baby spinach, wilted
and well-drained
1 small red chilli pepper, finely
sliced
55g (2oz) plant-based bacon or
salami-style slices
4 eggs
20g (¾oz) vegetarian Italian hard
cheese, finely grated
light-tasting oil, for drizzling
a handful of basil leaves
salt and black pepper

Preheat the oven to 220°C/430°F/gas 8 and put two
baking sheets inside to heat up.

Sprinkle the hot baking sheets with flour and lay the
pizza bases on them.

Spread the tomato passata thinly over the bases, leaving
a border around the edge. Scatter with the mozzarella,
spinach, chilli and plant-based bacon or salami. Make
two 'nests' in the topping of each pizza and crack an
egg into each. Finally, sprinkle over the hard cheese
and season with salt and pepper. Cook in the oven for
10–12 minutes, or according to the packet instructions.
Drizzle with light-tasting oil, tear over the basil leaves
and serve.

Italian 'meatball' &
RICE BROTH

Hearty and warming, this is a dinner you'll make over and over again. You can find lots of varieties of plant-based meatballs in most large supermarkets, if you want to make this more quickly.

 Serves:
4

 **Takes:**
35 minutes

For the 'meatballs' (or use shop-bought)
250g (9oz) plant-based mince
1 large garlic clove, crushed
50g (2oz) vegetarian Italian hard
   cheese (or vegan alternative),
   finely grated, plus extra to serve
35g (1¼oz) fresh breadcrumbs
1 egg, beaten
handful of parsley, finely chopped,
   plus extra to serve

For the broth
1.5l (6 cups) fresh vegetable stock
125g (scant ¾ cup) carnaroli rice
150g (5½oz) kale, chard, cavolo
   nero or other greens, tough stalks
   removed and roughly sliced
125g (4½oz) frozen peas
salt and black pepper

Combine the mince, garlic, hard cheese, breadcrumbs, egg, parsley and seasoning in a bowl and mix well. Shape the mixture into tiny meatballs about the size of a small cherry tomato.

Tip the stock into a saucepan and bring to the boil, add the rice and simmer for 5 minutes, then drop in the meatballs. Bring back to a gentle simmer and cook for 10 minutes. Add the greens and peas and cook for a further 5 minutes. Taste and season, then ladle into bowls and grate over some extra cheese before serving.

Spinach & ricotta
CRESPOLINI

Knowing how to make béchamel sauce is really handy – you can use it with all kinds of cheesy dishes like mac and cheese or lasagna.

 Serves:
4

 **Takes:**
1 hour 30 minutes, plus
30 minutes resting

8 crêpes (made following the recipe on page 170)

For the béchamel
750ml (3 cups) whole milk
60g (2oz) butter, plus extra for greasing
3 heaped tbsp plain (all-purpose) flour
½ tsp mustard powder (optional)
generous pinch of nutmeg
1½ tsp salt
black pepper

For the filling
300g (10oz) kale, Swiss chard leaves or other greens, torn and washed in cold water
300g (10oz) well-drained ricotta
2 small eggs, lightly beaten
60g (10oz) vegetarian Italian hard cheese, grated
grated zest of ½ lemon
90g (3oz) grated gruyère (or other cheese that melts well, such as cheddar)

Preheat the oven to 180°C/350°F/gas 4 and butter a 30x20cm (12x8in) baking dish.

To make the béchamel, heat the milk in a pan until steaming but not boiling. Remove from the heat. Melt the butter in a separate pan, add the flour and stir for 1 minute over a medium heat. Remove from the heat and gradually whisk in the warm milk until everything is combined. Return the pan to a low heat, add the mustard powder (if using), nutmeg and salt and black pepper. Simmer, stirring constantly, until thickened. Remove from the heat and add more salt and black pepper if needed. Spread the béchamel in the base of the prepared baking dish.

For the filling, place the greens in a large saucepan set over a medium heat, cover and cook for a few minutes until wilted. Drain well and, when cool enough to handle, squeeze out the excess liquid and finely chop. Place in a bowl along with the ricotta, eggs, half the hard cheese and the lemon zest. Season generously with salt and black pepper and mix well.

Divide the ricotta mixture equally between the crêpes and roll up into parcels. Arrange on top of the béchamel. Sprinkle over the gruyère and the remaining hard cheese. Bake for 25 minutes, or until the top is golden. Serve with a green salad.

Mulligatawny
SOUP

There are lots of variations on this curried soup, but with a well-stocked pantry, this is a winning, budget-friendly, healthy dinner. You'll need a hand blender to make it smooth.

 Serves:
6–8

 **Takes:**
about 1 hour

2 tbsp cooking oil
1 large onion, finely chopped
1 carrot, finely chopped
2 sticks celery, finely chopped
3 garlic cloves, finely chopped
4cm (1½in) piece of ginger, peeled
    and finely chopped
2 tsp garam masala
½ tsp turmeric
1½ tbsp curry powder
½ nutmeg, finely grated
125g (¾ cup) dried red lentils
550g (1lb 3oz) peeled and chopped
    butternut squash
2 tbsp tomato purée (paste)
1.2l (5 cups) vegetable stock
1 x 400ml (14fl oz) tin (can) coconut
    milk
175g (1 cup) jasmine rice
salt and black pepper

For the topping (optional)
1 green apple, cut into matchsticks
juice of ½ lime, plus lime wedges
50g (2oz) cashew nuts, toasted
handful of coriander (cilantro)
    leaves

Heat the oil in a large saucepan over a medium heat. Add the onion, carrot and celery and cook for about 8 minutes until softened. Stir through the garlic, ginger and spices and cook for 2 minutes more. Tip in the lentils, butternut squash and tomato purée and stir together. Pour over the stock and coconut milk, then bring to a simmer. Cover and cook for 30 minutes until the lentils and squash are soft. Leave to cool a little.

Meanwhile, cook the rice according to the packet instructions. Using a hand blender, blitz the soup together with half of the rice until smooth. Stir through the remaining unblended rice, adding a little more water if it's too thick. Season and warm through.

If you want to add the toppings, mix together the apple matchsticks and lime juice. Ladle the soup into bowls, top with the apple, cashew nuts and a few coriander leaves. Serve extra lime wedges on the side for squeezing over.

Chilli butter
SPRING GREEN PILAF

Using frozen baby broad (fava) beans makes this quicker. The chilli butter gives this the wow factor - you'll be adding it to everything.

 Serves:
4

 **Takes:**
40 minutes

280g (1½ cups) basmati rice
75g (2½oz) butter
2 leeks, thinly sliced
2 garlic cloves, crushed
½ tsp allspice
425ml (1¾ cups) hot vegetable
   stock
300g (10½oz) frozen podded baby
   broad (fava) beans, defrosted
250g (9oz) bunch of asparagus,
   sliced into 4cm (1½in) pieces
50g (2oz) pistachios, roughly
   chopped (optional)
½ small bunch of dill, finely
   chopped
salt and black pepper

To serve
Greek yoghurt
1½-2 tsp chilli (red pepper) flakes

Tip the rice into a bowl and cover with cold water. Meanwhile, heat 50g (2oz) of the butter in a large saucepan over a medium heat. Once foaming, add the leeks and cook for 8 minutes until softened. Stir through the garlic and allspice. Drain the rice, add it to the pan and stir to coat in the butter. Pour over the stock, season and bring to the boil, then reduce the heat to its lowest setting, cover and simmer for 10 minutes.

Quickly lift the lid and scatter over the broad beans and asparagus, cover and cook for a further 5 minutes. Remove from the heat and set aside to steam for 10 minutes.

Toast the pistachios, if using, in a frying pan. Stir the dill and pistachios into the rice. Divide between plates and top with a dollop of Greek yoghurt. Return the frying pan to the heat and add the final 25g (1oz) of butter. Once foaming, add the chilli flakes, sizzle for a moment, then pour a little over each plate.

Congee &
CRISPY FIVE-SPICE TOFU

Prepared all over Asia, congee is a popular porridge-like breakfast or late-supper dish. This version makes a comforting main, with the crispy tofu, spring onions and sesame seeds adding a satisfying crunch to the softness of the rice.

 Serves:
2

 Takes:
50 minutes

175g (generous ¾ cup) sushi or jasmine rice
1.2l (5 cups) vegetable stock
2 cloves garlic, finely grated
5cm (2in) piece of ginger, peeled and finely grated
175g (6oz) firm tofu
1 tsp Chinese five-spice powder
cooking oil
1 tbsp cornflour (cornstarch)
salt

To garnish
2 spring onions (scallions), white sliced, green shredded
2 tsp toasted sesame seeds
soy sauce

Wash the rice thoroughly. Tip the stock, garlic and ginger into a large saucepan and bring to the boil. Add the rice, bring back to the boil, then turn down the heat and simmer for 40 minutes, stirring occasionally. When cooked, the rice should be thick and porridge-like – add more water if needed.

Meanwhile, cut the tofu into 1.5–2cm (¾in) cubes, pat dry with paper towel and toss with the Chinese five-spice and some salt. Set aside for 30 minutes.

Heat a shallow layer of cooking oil in a frying pan over a high heat. Toss the tofu in the cornflour and fry in the hot oil for about 5 minutes until crispy all over. Ladle the congee into bowls, top with the tofu and garnish with the spring onions, sesame seeds and some soy sauce.

One-pan sauce with
FARFALLE & ROCKET

This sauce is a great, easy way to use up past-their-best veggies: pop them in a roasting tray with some herbs and seasoning, roast, add stock, whizz up and serve with pasta.

 Serves:
4–6

 Takes:
1¾ hours

2 red (bell) peppers, cored, deseeded and roughly chopped
2 red onions, chopped
2 carrots, peeled and chopped
3 garlic cloves, peeled
2 celery sticks, chopped
1 x 400g (14oz) tin (can) plum tomatoes
50g (2oz) sun-dried tomatoes in oil (drained weight)
2 tbsp cooking oil
2 tsp dried oregano
½ tsp chilli (red pepper) flakes
650ml (2¾ cups) hot vegetable stock
450g (1lb) dried farfalle
40g (1½oz) rocket (arugula)
salt and black pepper

Preheat the oven to 180°C/350°F/gas 4.

Put all the prepared veg in a large, deep roasting tray and add the tinned and sun-dried tomatoes. Drizzle over the oil, season well and sprinkle over the oregano and chilli flakes. Toss well and cook in the oven for 1 hour. Add the stock and return the tray to the oven for 30 minutes until the vegetables are tender. Use a hand blender to blitz, if you've got one, or leave chunky if you don't.

Meanwhile, cook the farfalle in a large pan of boiling, salted water, according to the packet instructions. Drain, reserving a cupful of the cooking water, and return the pasta to the pan. Tip in the sauce, adding a little pasta water if required. Mix together well and spoon into dishes, then top with the rocket and serve.

Nasi
GORENG

Meaning 'fried rice' in Indonesian, this dish is a flavour hit and packs a protein punch. Kecap manis is easily found in supermarkets these days. Leave out the egg to make this vegan.

 Serves:
2–3

 **Takes:**
35 minutes

150g (¾ cup) easy-cook long-grain
  rice (we used wholegrain)
3 tbsp cooking oil
5 spring onions (scallions),
  thinly sliced
3 garlic cloves, finely chopped
2½cm (1in) piece of ginger, peeled
  and finely grated
2 carrots, cut into matchsticks
200g (7oz) Chinese cabbage,
  thickly shredded
1 tsp chilli sauce such as sriracha,
  plus extra to serve
2 tsp tomato purée (paste)
1 tbsp soy sauce
1 tbsp kecap manis or thick, sweet
  soy sauce
75g (2½oz) frozen edamame beans
½ small bunch of coriander
  (cilantro), roughly chopped

To garnish
2-3 eggs
handful of roasted and salted
  peanuts, roughly chopped
  (optional)

Cook the rice according to the packet instructions. Heat 2 tablespoons of the oil in a large frying pan. Fry four of the spring onions, the garlic and the ginger for 2 minutes. Push to the side of the pan, add the carrots and cabbage and fry until softened.

Mix together the chilli sauce, tomato purée, soy sauce and kecap manis in a small bowl. Add this to the pan and bubble for a few moments, then stir through the cooked rice and edamame beans until warmed through. Add half the coriander.

Heat the remaining oil in a small frying pan and fry two or three eggs. Divide the rice between shallow bowls. Top with the fried eggs, the remaining coriander and spring onion and the peanuts and drizzle with chilli sauce.

Cheesy
COURGETTE GRATIN

This dish is great for using up courgettes and is hearty, warming and rich for a cold winter's day.

 Serves:
4

 **Takes:**
55 minutes

200g (1 cup) easy-cook
  wholegrain rice
25g (1oz) butter, plus extra
  for greasing
1 red onion, finely sliced
850g (1lb 14oz) courgettes
  (zucchinis), coarsely grated
2 garlic cloves, crushed
250g (9oz) mascarpone
100ml (scant ½ cup) milk
1 heaped tbsp dijon mustard
100g (3½oz) finely grated cheese
  that melts well such as cheddar or
  gruyère
salt and black pepper

*For the red onion and caper salad
(optional)*
½ red onion, finely chopped
1½ tbsp capers, roughly chopped
small bunch of flat-leaf parsley,
  finely chopped

Bring a large pan of salted water to the boil, tip in the rice and simmer for 15–20 minutes until almost fully cooked, then drain.

Meanwhile, heat the butter in a large frying pan and cook the onion for 8 minutes. Turn up the heat to the highest setting, add the courgettes and cook for 10 minutes. Stir in the garlic and some seasoning, then combine with the rice and set aside to cool.

Preheat the oven to 200°C/400°F/gas 6. In a bowl, mix together the mascarpone, milk, mustard, 75g (2½oz) of the cheese and some seasoning. Add to the rice and mix well. Transfer to a lightly buttered baking dish and top with the remaining cheese. Bake for 30 minutes until golden and bubbling.

Meanwhile, mix together the ingredients for the salad, if wanted, and serve alongside the gratin.

Chickpea & rice
STUFFED SQUASH

Pomegranate seeds pair so well with the squash and feta, but they are expensive. Leave them out, or treat yourself, then make the recipe on page 55 the following day to use them all up.

 Serves:
2

 **Takes:**
45 minutes

100g (½ cup plus 1 tbsp) rice (we used basmati and wild rice)
1 small butternut squash or other small, seasonal squash such as onion or kabocha
1 tbsp cooking oil
100g (3½oz) tinned (canned) chickpeas (drained weight)
1 small red onion, finely chopped
25g (1oz) pomegranate seeds (optional)
25g (1oz) hazelnuts, toasted and roughly chopped (optional)
½ tsp ground cumin
zest of ½ orange
½ small bunch of dill, roughly chopped (optional)
½ small bunch of parsley, roughly chopped
50g (2oz) feta
salt and pepper

For the tahini dressing
1 small garlic clove, crushed
3 tbsp tahini
juice of ½ orange
salt and pepper

Cook the rice in salted water according to the packet instructions. Drain, then spread it out on a tray and leave to cool.

Meanwhile, preheat the oven to 200°C/400°F/gas 6. Halve the squash and scrape out the seeds (use a very sharp knife to do this, and watch your fingers!). Rub all over, even the skin, with the oil. Season and roast, cut-side up, for 30-40 minutes, or until tender.

Combine the rice, chickpeas, onion, pomegranate seeds and hazelnuts, if using, cumin, orange zest, herbs and seasoning in a bowl. In a separate bowl, mix together the garlic, tahini and orange juice with some seasoning and enough cold water to make a drizzly dressing – about 1-2 tablespoons. Pile the rice into the roasted squash halves, crumble over the feta and drizzle with the tahini dressing.

Aloo gobi
TAHARI

A one-pot rice pilaf, full of vegetable-y goodness and super filling thanks to the potatoes.

 Serves:
2

 **Takes:**
50 minutes

1½ tbsp ghee or oil
1 large red onion, sliced
1 tsp black mustard seeds
1 tsp cumin seeds
200g (7oz) potatoes, cut into
   2.5–3cm (1in) chunks
150g (5½oz) cauliflower florets
2 garlic cloves, crushed
1 tsp freshly grated ginger
2 tomatoes, roughly chopped
2 tsp curry powder
100g (½ cup plus 1 tbsp)
   basmati rice
50g (2oz) frozen peas, defrosted
300ml (1¼ cups) boiling water
25g (1oz) cashew nuts, roughly
   crushed (optional)
salt and black pepper
raita, to serve

Heat 1 tablespoon of the ghee or oil in a large frying pan over a medium-high heat. Add the onion and a pinch of salt and cook for 10 minutes until golden brown. Add the mustard and cumin seeds and fry until popping. Remove using a slotted spoon and set aside.

Add the remaining ghee to the pan and fry the potatoes and cauliflower for 5 minutes, or until starting to brown. Stir through the garlic and ginger, then the tomatoes and cook for 1 minute. Add the curry powder, rice and some seasoning and stir to coat. Add the peas, half the cooked onion and the boiling water. Cover and simmer over the lowest heat for 15 minutes, or until the rice and potatoes are cooked and the water has been absorbed. Turn off the heat and leave to steam for 10 minutes

Meanwhile, toast the crushed cashews in a small frying pan. Fluff the rice before serving topped with the reserved onion, crumbled cashews and some raita.

Mujadara
RICE

An earthy Lebanese rice dish. Any leftovers are delicious cold the following day – why not take this to the library for an easy but nutritious lunch?

Serves:
4–5

Takes:
45 minutes,
plus steaming

175g (1 cup) jasmine or
  basmati rice
6 tbsp sunflower oil
4 onions, thinly sliced
4 garlic cloves, thinly sliced
2 tsp ground cumin
2 tsp ground coriander
1 tsp ground cinnamon
1 x 400g (14oz) tin (can) brown
  lentils, rinsed and drained
300ml (1¼ cups) hot vegetable
  stock
4-5 tbsp Greek-style yoghurt or
  vegan alternative
handful of mint leaves, roughly torn
  (optional)
salt and black pepper

Soak the rice in plenty of cold water. Meanwhile, heat half the oil in a large frying pan over a high heat. Fry half the onions with a pinch of salt for about 15 minutes, until caramelized and crispy. Remove using a slotted spoon and spread out on paper towel. Repeat with the remaining oil and onions.

Add the garlic and spices to the oil in the pan and cook for 30 seconds. Tip in the lentils and drained rice. Stir to coat, then pour over the stock and add one-third of the fried onions. Cover and simmer for 10 minutes, then turn off the heat and steam for 10 minutes. Season, fluff with a fork and transfer to a serving plate. Dollop and drizzle over the yoghurt, then scatter over the remaining onions, mint and a grinding of black pepper.

Vegan
RAGÙ

This vegan ragù, like most deep, rich sauces and stews, is best served up the next day after marinating in the fridge. The perfect lunch to reheat on campus!

 Serves:
6–8

 Takes:
1½ hours

2 tbsp cooking oil
2 onions, finely chopped
2 carrots, peeled and finely chopped
2 celery sticks, finely chopped
3 garlic cloves, peeled
2 bay leaves
2 sprigs of rosemary
2 sprigs of thyme
300g (10oz) mushrooms, finely chopped
3 tbsp tomato purée (paste)
250ml (1 cup) red wine
1 x 400g (14oz) tin (can) brown lentils
70g (2½ cup) walnut halves or brazil nuts, chopped
40g (2oz) black olives, pitted and chopped (optional)
1 tbsp vegan Worcestershire sauce
salt and black pepper
100g (3½oz) dried pasta per person (we used rigatoni)
freshly grated vegan Italian hard cheese

Place a large pan over a low heat. Add the oil and tip in the chopped vegetables, garlic and herbs. Gently fry for 10 minutes until softened but not golden.

Add the mushrooms and cook for a further 10 minutes, then stir in the tomato purée. Turn up the heat and add the wine. Allow to bubble for 2 minutes.

Tip in the can of lentils with their liquid, then add the nuts, olives (if using) and Worcestershire sauce. Reduce the heat and simmer for 1 hour or until thickened, stirring occasionally. Season to taste and remove any herb stalks.

Serve with penne or rigatoni, sprinkled with grated Italian hard cheese. Any sauce you are not using straight away can be stored in the fridge or frozen.

Caribbean
RICE & PEAS

A staple of the Caribbean diet, rice and peas is enjoyed all over the world. It goes with everything. Remember to cool leftover rice quickly and only reheat it once.

 Serves:
4

 **Takes:**
35 minutes

5 spring onions (scallions), finely sliced
1 whole chilli (we used scotch bonnet for a fiery hit)
2 garlic cloves, peeled and bashed
4 large thyme sprigs, plus extra to garnish
½ heaped tsp allspice
250g (1¼ cups) easy-cook long-grain rice
1 x 400ml (14fl oz) tin (can) coconut milk
250ml (1 cup) hot vegetable stock
½ tsp salt
1 x 400g (14oz) tin (can) kidney beans, rinsed and drained

Tip the spring onions, chilli, garlic, thyme, allspice and rice into a large saucepan. Pour over the coconut milk and stir. Add the vegetable stock and salt, then bring to the boil. Turn down the heat to its lowest setting, cover and simmer for 10 minutes.

Quickly lift the lid and add the kidney beans, cover and cook for a further 10 minutes. Turn off the heat and set aside, covered, for 10 minutes. Stir and serve topped with a few sprigs of thyme.

Simple
TOMATO SAUCE

This is the most simple pasta sauce recipe. It's a great starting point if you've never made a pasta sauce from scratch before, and it's ideal for freezing into portions.

 Serves:
10–12

 **Takes:**
1 hour 30 minutes

2 tbsp cooking oil
4 onions, finely chopped
3 garlic cloves, sliced
10g (⅓oz) basil, leaves picked and stalks chopped
3 fresh bay leaves
4 x 400g (14oz) tins (cans) plum tomatoes, or 2 x 680g (24oz) jars passata (strained tomatoes)
salt and black pepper

To serve
linguine (allow 100g/3½oz dried per person)
freshly grated vegetarian Italian hard cheese

Place a large saucepan over a low heat. Add the oil, onions, garlic, chopped basil stalks and bay leaves, along with a good pinch of salt. Sauté for 20 minutes or until softened but not coloured, stirring occasionally.

Open the cans of tomatoes, if using, and chop the tomatoes in the cans using a pair of kitchen scissors. Tip the tomatoes or passata (strained tomatoes) into the pan, followed by half a tomato tin or a quarter of a passata jar of water, swirling it around first to get everything out. Turn up the heat, then reduce to a simmer. Cook the sauce for around 1 hour with a lid on, slightly ajar.

Season to taste and take off the heat. You can keep the sauce slightly chunky or blitz to your desired consistency in using a hand blender once cooled (removing the bay leaves first).

Serve tossed through linguine, topped with the basil leaves and a good grating of hard cheese.

Roasted tomato & cannellini
COURGETTI

Using 'courgetti' instead of the pasta makes this three of your five-a-day in just one meal, but you can use regular spaghetti, if you prefer.

 Serves:
2

 Takes:
35 minutes

250g (9oz) small tomatoes (we used cherry tomatoes)
1 garlic clove, crushed
1 tsp dried thyme
½ lemon
½ tsp coriander seeds
½ x 400g (14oz) tin (can) cannellini beans
1 tbsp cooking oil
15g (1 tbsp) pine nuts (optional)
250g (9oz) shop-bought courgetti (zoodles) (or use 200g/7oz dried pasta)
salt and black pepper

To serve
light-tasting oil
large handful of watercress

Preheat the oven to 180°C/350°F/gas 4.

Place the tomatoes in a large roasting tray. Add the garlic and sprinkle over the thyme. Using a swivel peeler, pare three strips of zest from the lemon and add to the tray, along with the coriander seeds. Drain the beans into a sieve, rinse, pat dry with paper towel and add to the tray. Add the oil and season with salt and pepper. Toss everything together and cook in the oven for 25 minutes, adding the pine nuts (if using) for the final 5 minutes.

Meanwhile, place the courgetti in a microwave-proof bowl and cover with a clean damp cloth.

When the tomatoes are juicy and cooked down, and the beans are golden and crisp, remove the tray from the oven. Microwave the courgetti on high for 2 minutes (or alternatively you can keep them raw, or stir-fry briefly in 1 teaspoon of cooking oil). Give everything in the roasting tray a quick toss, then tip in the courgetti. Toss again, divide between bowls, drizzle with light-tasting oil and top with watercress.

Fresh, green open
LASAGNE

This is a simple way of making a lasagne-style dish without the baking. The green vegetables make it a perfect summer supper.

 Serves:
2

 Takes:
30 minutes

100g (3½oz) mascarpone
70g (2½oz) soft goats' cheese
40g (1½oz) vegetarian Italian hard cheese, freshly grated
20ml (4 tsp) milk
pinch of dried nutmeg
1 tbsp cooking oil, plus extra for drizzling
2 shallots, sliced
70g (2½oz) fine asparagus, stalks sliced and tips left whole
100g (3½oz) frozen broad (fava) beans, skins removed
70g (2½ cup) frozen peas
grated zest and juice of ½ lemon
4 fresh lasagne sheets
3 tbsp vegetarian green pesto
salt and black pepper

Get a large saucepan of salted water on to boil for the lasagne.

Spoon the mascarpone, goats' cheese, hard cheese and milk into a saucepan over a very low heat. Stir and allow the cheeses to melt, then season with a little salt and pepper. Remove the bowl from the heat and add the nutmeg.

Place a large frying pan on a medium heat. Add the oil and shallots and sauté for 5 minutes until softened, then add the asparagus tips and sliced stalks, the broad beans and peas. Sauté for a further 2 minutes, then add the lemon zest and juice, season and take off the heat.

Cook the lasagne in the pan of boiling, salted water, according to the packet instructions. Drain and place on a tray, then drizzle with olive oil.

Working quickly, get your serving plates ready. Place a spoonful of cheese sauce on each plate. Drape a lasagne sheet over the sauce and spoon over some vegetables, then more sauce and a little pesto. Top with a lasagne sheet and finish with more sauce and pesto. Repeat with the other plate and serve.

Spicy chickpea &
SWEET POTATO PENNE

This chickpea and sweet potato sauce transforms into a comforting stew when served with crusty bread in place of the pasta.

 Serves:
4–6

 Takes:
1¼ hours

700g (1lb 9oz) sweet potatoes, peeled
2 tbsp cooking oil
2 onions, sliced
2 garlic cloves, sliced
1 tsp dried rosemary
pinch of chilli (red pepper) flakes
1 x 400g (14oz) tin (can) chickpeas
300g (10oz) dried pasta (we used wholewheat penne)
100g (3½oz) kale, leaves torn from the stalks and finely sliced
juice of ½ lemon
salt and black pepper

To serve
40g (1½oz) feta (optional)
light-tasting oil

Coarsely grate the sweet potatoes.

Place a large frying pan on a medium heat and add the oil. Add the onions, garlic and rosemary and gently fry for 10 minutes until softened. Add the grated sweet potato and chilli flakes and cook for 20 minutes until it has reduced. Tip in the chickpeas (with their liquid) and bring to the boil. Reduce the heat, cover and simmer gently for 25 minutes.

Before the end of the simmering time, cook the pasta in a large pan of boiling, salted water, according to the packet instructions. Add a ladle of the pasta cooking water to the sweet potato mixture. To make this silky smooth, use a hand blender, if you've got one, to blitz half the mixture until smooth (if you don't, it'll just be a bit more rustic). Add the kale and simmer until wilted.

Drain the pasta and tip into the frying pan. Toss well, add the lemon juice and season to taste. Divide between dishes, crumble over the feta, if using, and drizzle over a little light-tasting oil to serve.

Vegan
CARBONARA

This carbonara is non-traditional but delicious, and comes with a protein hit from the tofu and nutritional yeast. Dare we say it's better than the original?! You'll need a hand blender for this recipe.

 Serves:
2

 Takes:
30 minutes,
plus soaking

75g (2½oz) cashew nuts
2 tbsp cooking oil
225g (8oz) smoked tofu, cut into
2cm (¾in) pieces
250ml (1 cup) unsweetened nut
milk (cashew or almond work
best)
1 tsp light soy sauce
2 tbsp nutritional yeast, plus
extra to serve
1 red onion, chopped
2 garlic cloves, crushed
10g (⅓oz) flat-leaf parsley,
leaves and stalks chopped
(kept separate)
125g (4½oz) mushrooms, sliced
200g (7oz) dried spaghetti
salt and black pepper

Put the cashews in a small bowl, cover with cold water and set aside to soak for 20 minutes.

Meanwhile, heat the oil in a large frying pan over a medium-high heat. Add the tofu and sauté for 5 minutes until golden and crisp. Remove the pan from the heat, spoon the tofu on to a plate and place to one side.

Drain the cashew nuts and, using a hand blender, blitz with the nut milk, soy sauce and nutritional yeast until smooth, then season.

Place the frying pan back on the heat. Add the onion, garlic and chopped parsley stalks with a pinch of salt and sauté for 5-10 minutes until softened. Add the mushrooms and fry for a further 5-10 minutes, season, then turn the heat down low.

Meanwhile, cook the pasta in a large pan of boiling, salted water according to the packet instructions. Drain, reserving a cupful of cooking water, and tip into the frying pan with the tofu and sauce. Toss together well, adding a little pasta water if needed. Sprinkle in the chopped parsley leaves and divide between plates. Sprinkle over a little more nutritional yeast and some black pepper, and serve.

Sweet potato & ricotta
GRATINATED CRÊPES

Sweet potato, ricotta and sage are a classic flavour combination. Crêpes are easy to fill and roll, and they give this a lovely texture.

 Serves:
6–8

 Takes:
1 hour 30 minutes, plus
30 minutes resting

800g (1lb 12oz) sweet potatoes, peeled and cut into 2cm (¾in) cubes
2 tbsp cooking oil
salt and black pepper

For the filling
60ml (¼ cup) cooking oil
2 onions, finely chopped
salt
2 garlic cloves, finely chopped
200g (7oz) ricotta
70g (2½oz) vegetarian Italian hard cheese, grated
40g (1¼oz) toasted pine nuts (optional)
finely grated zest of 1 lemon
pinch of nutmeg
3 tbsp double cream

For the sage butter (optional)
4 tbsp butter
8 large sage leaves
1 tsp lemon juice

8 crêpes (made following the recipe on page 170)

Preheat the oven to 230°C/450°F/gas 8. Spread the sweet potatoes in a single layer on a baking tray, toss with the oil and season. Roast for 25–30 minutes, or until tender and brown at the edges.

To make the filling, heat the oil in a frying pan, add the onions and a pinch of salt and gently fry for 8 minutes, or until very soft but not coloured. Add the garlic and fry for 2 more minutes. Set aside to cool. In a mixing bowl, stir together the ricotta, 20g (¾oz) of the hard cheese and all the remaining filling ingredients, including the cooled onions. Set aside.

For the sage butter, melt the butter in a pan and let it bubble over a medium heat until it turns golden and smells toasty. Add the sage and lemon juice and keep warm over a very low heat.

Preheat the grill to high. Butter a baking dish 30x20cm (12x8in) or similar.

Distribute the ricotta mixture and sweet potatoes between the crêpes and roll up, transferring to the baking dish as you go. Brush the tops of the pancakes with the sage butter and sprinkle with the remaining cheese. Grill for 4–5 minutes (about 10cm/4in below the grill), or until golden. Serve hot, with more butter spooned over.

Squash & brussels sprouts
PENNE

Butternut squash and brussels sprouts add a warming, autumnal touch to this lightly spiced pasta. Keep leftover sauce in the fridge for 1-2 days and reheat as needed.

 Serves:
4–6

 Takes:
1 hour

900g (2lb) butternut squash
1 tsp ground cinnamon
1 tsp sweet smoked paprika
2 tbsp cooking oil
2 red onions, sliced
200g (7oz) brussels sprouts
1 tsp maple syrup
1 tbsp light soy sauce
300g (10oz) dried pasta (we used penne)
35g (1¼oz) vegetarian Italian hard cheese, freshly grated, plus extra to serve (optional)
salt and black pepper

Preheat the oven to 180°C/350°F/gas 4. Peel the butternut squash, halve (you'll need a very sharp knife for this - keep your fingers out of the way!) and scoop out the seeds. Rinse the seeds under the tap, dry on paper towel and spread out on a roasting tray. Season and add a pinch each of the cinnamon and smoked paprika. Drizzle with 1 tablespoon of the oil and toss together.

Cut the squash into 2cm (¾in) cubes. Place in a large roasting tray with the sliced onions. Season, drizzle with the remaining oil and sprinkle over the remaining spices. Toss together and roast for 40 minutes. Roast the seeds at the same time until golden and crisp, which should take around 20 minutes.

Finely slice the sprouts. Once the squash is cooked, stir in the sprouts, maple syrup and soy sauce, then roast for a further 10 minutes.

Meanwhile, cook the pasta in a large pan of boiling, salted water, according to the packet instructions. Drain, reserving a cupful of the pasta water, and tip into the roasting tray with the squash. Toss with the hard cheese and a little pasta water if needed. Season to taste, divide between bowls and sprinkle over the roasted seeds and a little extra cheese, if you like.

DESSERT

Strawberry
FRENCH TOAST

Pain perdu is traditionally made with slightly stale bread, which helps to soak up more of the egg batter. You can use brioche or even leftover Christmas panettone in place of the bread.

 Serves:
4

 **Takes:**
10 minutes

200g (7oz) strawberries, hulled and cut in half
2 tbsp caster (superfine) sugar
150g (5½oz) raspberries
3 eggs
100ml (scant ½ cup) full-fat (whole) milk
4 thick slices of leftover bread, at least a day old (we used panettone)
20g (¾oz) butter
icing (confectioner's) sugar, to dust
maple syrup or honey, to drizzle
mascarpone, Greek yoghurt or ice cream, to serve (optional)

Place the strawberries in a small pan with the sugar and heat gently until the sugar has dissolved. Stir through the raspberries and continue to cook for a couple of minutes, until they start to release their juices. Remove and set aside.

Mix the eggs and milk together in a shallow bowl and soak two slices of bread on each side. Heat half the butter in a large frying pan, add the soaked bread and fry over a medium heat for 2 minutes on each side, until golden and crisp. Remove and dust with icing (confectioner's) sugar. Repeat the soaking and frying with the remaining two slices.

Place a slice of French toast on each plate, spoon the syrupy berries over the top, drizzle with the maple syrup and serve with mascarpone, Greek yoghurt or ice cream, if you like.

Mango & lime
ETON MESS

Eton mess sounds fancy but it's basically just a construction job. The cardamom and honey are a delicious combo but feel free to use whichever fruit you like best.

 Serves:
4

 Takes:
15 minutes

2 ripe mangoes
juice and zest of 1 lime
2 tbsp runny honey
1 cardamom pod, seeds removed
   and crushed
250ml (1 cup) double (heavy) cream
4 tsp icing (confectioner's) sugar
4 meringue nests
chopped pistachios, to garnish
   (optional)
few small mint leaves, to garnish
   (optional)

Peel the mangoes, cut the flesh away from the stones and chop. Place three-quarters of the mango flesh in a bowl and add half the lime juice and all of the zest. Using a hand blender, blitz the remaining mango and lime juice with the honey, crushed cardamom and 1 tablespoon of water to form a smooth purée.

Whip the cream and icing (confectioner's) sugar in a bowl to form soft peaks. Break the meringues into chunky pieces and fold through the cream along with the mango purée. Spoon between four bowls, add the chopped mango and scatter with the pistachios and mint leaves, if using.

Cheat's
CUSTARD TARTS

The flavour of these tarts depends on the taste of your custard – so use fresh, if you can. You'll need a muffin tin for this recipe.

 Makes:
10

 **Takes:**
I hour, plus cooling

400g (14oz) vanilla custard
   (preferably fresh)
2 egg yolks
butter, to grease
300g (10½oz) ready-made all-butter
   puff pastry

Thoroughly whisk the egg yolks into the custard. Set aside.

Grease 10 holes of a 12-hole muffin tin generously with butter and chill.

Roll the pastry out into a long rectangle of about 40x18cm (16x7in), and roll up from the short end into a tight log. Cut into 10x1.5cm (4x½in) rounds (discarding the ends) and roll each out into a 10cm (4in) disc. Use these to line your muffin tin and chill until needed.

Preheat the oven to 250°C/480°F/gas 9 and place a baking sheet inside. Divide the custard between the pastry cases (leaving a 1cm/½ inch gap between the top of the filling and the pastry). Transfer to the preheated baking tray and bake for 18–20 minutes, until the pastry is crisp and the custard just set. Remove from the oven and leave for 5 minutes then carefully loosen with a knife and cool completely on a wire rack.

Chocolate & berry
VEGAN PANCAKES

Sneaky. Inside these tender, spongy pancakes is a hidden trove of melted chocolate and berries. No-one will ever know.

 Makes:
about 4
pancakes

 **Takes:**
30 minutes

1 tbsp ground flax seeds (linseeds)
200ml (generous ¾ cup) almond
  milk
1 tbsp lemon juice
1 tbsp melted coconut oil,
  cooled, plus extra for frying
150g (1¼ cups) plain
  (all-purpose) white or
  wholemeal flour
1 heaped tbsp caster
  (superfine) sugar
1 tsp baking powder
½ tsp bicarbonate of soda (baking
  soda)
pinch salt
handful of blueberries (fresh or
  frozen)
60g (2oz) vegan dark chocolate,
  ideally in 10g (⅓oz) squares

In a small bowl, mix the flax seeds with 3 tablespoons of cold water and set aside for 10 minutes to thicken. Meanwhile, combine the almond milk, lemon juice and coconut oil in a jug.

In a mixing bowl, whisk together the flour, sugar, baking powder, bicarbonate of soda and salt, and make a well in the centre. Pour the soaked flax seeds into the well and then gradually stir in the milk mixture, incorporating the flour as you go, to produce a thick batter. You might not need all the milk. Be careful not to overmix; some small lumps are fine.

Heat a non-stick frying pan over a medium heat and brush generously with coconut oil. Drop dessertspoonfuls of the batter into the pan to make 8cm (3in) panckes. Cook for 30 seconds–1 minute.

Continues overleaf

Chocolate & berry vegan pancakes
continued...

Working quickly, drop a few blueberries into the centre of each pancake and top with a chocolate square. Spoon just enough batter on top to cover the chocolate and blueberries. Cook for a further 1 minute or so until golden underneath – make sure the heat is not too high or they will burn before they cook through. Flip and cook for a further 2 minutes.

Delicious served warm while the chocolate is oozy, but still very tasty served at room temperature.

Baby
BANOFFEE PIES

The original banoffee pie had coffee as well as toffee to thank for its name!

 Serves:
6

 Takes:
3 hours 25 minutes,
plus cooling

180g (6¼oz) digestive biscuits
   (graham crackers)
2 tbsp walnuts, finely chopped
1 tsp instant coffee powder
100g (3½oz) salted butter, melted,
   plus extra for greasing
1 x 397g (14oz) tin (can) caramel
   dessert filling
½ tsp salt
2–3 small/medium bananas
300ml (1¼ cups) double (heavy)
   cream
100g (3½oz) milk chocolate

Take a 12-hole muffin tin and lightly grease the base and sides of 6 of the holes. Cut out six circles of greaseproof paper and line the base of each.

Place the digestive biscuits, chopped walnuts and coffee in a ziplock back and roll with a rolling pin or, if you don't have one, a clean glass bottle, until you have crumbs with a sandy texture. You may need to do this in batches. Tip into a bowl, stir in the melted butter and mix well.

Divide the mixture between the muffin holes. Pat down with a spoon and use your fingers to press the mixture over the bases and up the sides of the holes. Place in the fridge to firm up for at least 1 hour.

Take the pie cases from the fridge and divide the caramel between them (you may have a little left over), allowing it to come just under the rims. Sprinkle each with a little salt and place the muffin tin back in the fridge if not serving straightaway. The cases can happily sit in the fridge for up to 24 hours.

Continues overleaf

Baby banoffee pies
continued...

Carefully remove the pie cases from the tin, removing the lining paper, and place on serving plates. When you're ready to serve, peel and slice the bananas into thin rounds. Arrange them over the top of the caramel.

Pour the double cream into a mixing bowl and whip to soft peaks. Spoon the cream over the top of each pie, grate over some chocolate and serve.

Mascarpone
BLUEBERRY CRÊPES

Why go out for pancakes when you can make these at home?!
Customize to your heart's content: ice cream, strawberry jam,
maple syrup...

 Makes:
10 crêpes

 **Takes:**
1 hour, plus 30
minutes resting

For the crêpes
130g (4½oz/1 cup) plain
   (all-purpose) or wholemeal plain
   flour
1 tbsp caster (superfine) sugar (omit
   for savoury recipes)
½ tsp sea salt
1 egg, lightly beaten
300ml (1¼ cups) full-fat (whole) milk
1 tbsp butter, melted and cooled
melted butter or vegetable oil,
   for frying

For the topping
250g (9oz) mascarpone
250ml (1 cup) double (heavy) cream
1 tbsp icing (confectioner's) sugar
1 tsp vanilla extract
blueberry compote

To make the crêpes, whisk together the flour, sugar and salt in a mixing bowl and make a well in the centre. In a jug, whisk together the egg, milk and melted butter. Gradually pour the egg mixture into the well and whisk, incorporating the flour as you go, to make a smooth batter. Don't overmix or the crêpes will be tough. Leave to stand for at least 30 minutes. The batter will thicken over this time, so stir in 1–2 tablespoons of cold water before cooking.

Heat a non-stick frying pan over a medium heat and when hot enough – a sprinkle of water should sizzle – add a little butter or oil and swirl around the pan. Pour 60ml (¼ cup) of batter into the pan, quickly swirling the pan to cover the base. Cook for 1–2 minutes until the edges of the crêpe look dry and the underneath is golden. Loosen the edges with a palette knife or spatula, flip and cook for a further 1–2 minutes. Repeat with the remaining batter.

To make the cream, briefly whisk the mascarpone to loosen. Add the cream, then whisk until light and fluffy. Stir in the icing sugar and vanilla.

To serve, spoon some of the mascarpone cream along the centre of a crêpe and roll up. Spoon over some of the blueberry compote and serve immediately.

Maple apple
'TARTE TATIN'

Traditional tarte tatin involves making pastry from scratch. This recipe takes out all the hard bits but keeps the delicious flavours.

 Serves:
6

 **Takes:**
50 minutes

150g (5oz/1¼ cups) plain (all-purpose) flour
1 tsp baking powder
½ tsp bicarbonate of soda
½ tsp sea salt
3 heaped tbsp caster (superfine) sugar
250ml (8½fl oz/1 cup) buttermilk (or see tip on page 97)
1 large egg, lightly beaten
1 tbsp melted butter
melted butter or vegetable oil, for frying
1 tsp vanilla extract
5 medium eating apples
60g (2oz) butter
90ml (⅓ cup) maple syrup
squeeze of lemon juice
250ml (1 cup) double (heavy) cream
1 tsp ground cinnamon

In a mixing bowl, whisk together the flour, baking powder, bicarbonate of soda, salt and sugar, and make a well in the centre. In a jug, whisk together the buttermilk, egg and melted butter. Gradually pour the egg mixture into the well and whisk, incorporating the flour as you go, to make a smooth batter. Finally, stir in the vanilla. Don't overmix: some small lumps are fine.

Preheat the oven to 220°C/425°F/gas 7.

Peel, core and quarter the apples, then cut each quarter in half. Melt the butter until foaming in an ovenproof, 15cm- (6in-) diameter frying pan. Add the apples, maple syrup and lemon juice and stir to combine. Simmer over a medium heat for about 10 minutes until the apples have softened and the liquid has reduced to a syrup: there should be plenty of syrup in the pan.

Take the pan off the heat and spread the pancake batter over the top with a spatula, making sure it completely covers the apples. Bake in the preheated oven for about 15 minutes, until golden and cooked through. Meanwhile, whip together the cream and cinnamon.

When the pancake is cooked, carefully invert it on to a plate. Cut into slices and serve warm with a generous spoonful of the cinnamon cream.

Crispy chocolate
& COCONUT BARS

This is a grown up version of chocolate rice crispy cakes, with loads of coconutty goodness.

Makes:
15 bars

Takes:
20 minutes,
plus chilling

150g (5½oz cups) puffed rice cereal
2½ tbsp coconut oil
100g (3½oz) honey or maple syrup
125g (4½oz) almond butter
3 tbsp cocoa powder
pinch of salt

For the topping
2½ tbsp coconut oil
200g (7oz) 70% dark chocolate
25g (1oz) desiccated (dried
   shredded) coconut
salt

Lightly grease and line a 20cm (8in) square tin with baking parchment. Tip the puffed rice into a large bowl. In a small pan, melt together the oil, honey or maple syrup, almond butter, cocoa powder and salt, stirring until smooth. Pour over the cereal and stir to coat. Transfer to the prepared tin and push down firmly with the back of a spoon to level. Chill for 30 minutes.

For the topping, melt together the oil and chocolate until smooth, either in the microwave or in a heatproof bowl over a pan of simmering water. Pour over the chilled base, then scatter the desiccated coconut and a little salt on top. Chill for 30 minutes or until firm, then cut into bars.

Chocolate chip cookies &
ICE CREAM

Because everybody needs a fail-safe chocolate chip cookie recipe. The best thing about these cookies is that they freeze really well – then simply bake from frozen whenever you want fresh cookies.

 Serves:
8

 **Takes:**
25 minutes,
plus chilling and cooling

125g (4½oz) unsalted butter
100g (3½oz) caster (superfine) sugar
150g (5½oz) light brown soft sugar
1 large egg
1 tsp vanilla extract
½ tsp salt
225g (8oz) plain (all-purpose) flour
½ tsp bicarbonate of soda (baking soda)
100g (3½oz) dark chocolate chips
50g (2oz) milk chocolate chips
ice cream, to serve

Preheat the oven to 180°C/350°F/gas 4. Line two baking sheets with parchment and set aside.

Melt the butter in a small pan or in the microwave, then transfer to a large mixing bowl. Add both types of sugar, the egg, vanilla and salt, and stir until the mixture is fully combined and smooth. Tip in the flour and bicarbonate of soda, gently folding into the wet ingredients and being careful not to overmix, then stir in the chocolate chips.

Use a couple of dessertspoons to scoop the mixture onto the prepared trays; you should get 16 cookies. Leave plenty of room for the cookies to spread during cooking.

Bake for 12–15 minutes until the edges are light golden. Leave to cool and set on the tray for 10 minutes, then transfer to a wire rack and allow to cool completely.

Sandwich two cookies together with a scoop of your favourite ice cream. Eat immediately.

Mascarpone & cherry jam
BRIOCHE

These brioche 'sandwiches' are an easy but delicious dessert when you're in the mood for something a little bit fancy.

 Serves:
8

 Takes:
10 minutes

8 chocolate chip brioche rolls
250g (9oz) mascarpone cheese
1 tsp vanilla extract
1 tbsp icing (confectioner's) sugar
1-2 tbsp milk
jar of cherry jam (jelly)

Preheat the oven to 180°C/350°F/gas 4. Heat the brioche rolls for 5 minutes.

Meanwhile, tip the mascarpone into a mixing bowl and stir in the vanilla, icing sugar and enough milk to loosen the mascarpone so that it is spreadable.

Split the brioche rolls in half. Spread the bottom half with mascarpone, spoon over some cherry jam and sandwich with the remaining half. Serve immediately.

Jam
TARTS

Jam tarts are a classic for a reason. They're so easy to make for a little treat. If you want to make these vegan, ensure the pastry is made with margarine or vegetable oils, and use jam in place of the curd.

 Makes:
18 tarts

 Takes:
30 minutes,
plus chilling

butter or oil, for greasing
1 x 320g (11oz) roll ready-made
   shortcrust pastry
125g (4½oz) fruit jam (jelly)
   or curd

Preheat the oven to 180°C/350°F/gas mark 4.

Lightly grease the holes of two 12-hole shallow cake tins. Roll the pastry out to about 5mm (¼in) thick. Take a 7cm (3in) round or fluted pastry cutter and cut out 18 rounds. If you don't have one, a cup or glass will do the trick. You may need to re-roll the pastry to make all 18. Use any leftover pastry to cut out decorations for the top of your tarts. Line the holes of the tin with the pastry circles and fill each with 1-2 tsp jam or curd. Put any pastry decorations on top.

Bake the tarts in the oven for about 15 minutes or until the jam bubbles a little. Remove from the oven and transfer to a wire rack. Be sure these have cooled before you eat them, otherwise the filling will burn your mouth.

Salted caramel & ice cream
WAFFLES

Quick, simple and delicious, this is a dangerously tempting dessert – promise us you won't eat it EVERY day!

 Serves:
2

 Takes:
15 minutes

25g (1oz) pecans
knob of very soft unsalted butter
pinch of salt
4 shop-bought Belgian butter
    waffles
2 scoops vanilla ice cream
2 tbsp ready-made salted caramel
    sauce

Preheat the oven to 180°C/350°F/gas 4.

Put the pecans on a large tray, dot over the butter and sprinkle with a pinch of salt. Bake for 5 minutes, then give the nuts a shake and push to one side. Lay the waffles on the tray and return to the oven for 5 more minutes. The nuts should be fragrant and the waffles just warm. Remove from the oven.

Put a waffle on to each serving plate and top with a scoop of ice cream. Drizzle with the caramel sauce, then roughly crush the nuts with your hands and sprinkle over the top. Sandwich with the remaining waffles and serve immediately.

No-bake
OREO PEANUT TART

This is so simple to make, with no baking required – an impressive dessert for birthdays or celebrations. It can easily be made vegan-friendly with a few substitutions.

 Serves:
16

 Takes:
30 minutes, plus chilling and setting

For the base
2 x 154g (5½oz) packs Oreo cookies (no need to remove the cream – it helps bind the base)
75g (2½oz) salted butter or vegan alternative, melted
2 tbsp crunchy peanut butter

For the filling
300ml (1¼ cups) double (heavy) cream
1 tsp cornflour (cornstarch)
250g (9oz) dark chocolate, finely chopped
50g (2oz) unsalted butter, softened
2 tbsp whole milk
pinch of salt
150g (5oz) roasted unsalted peanuts, finely chopped
4 tbsp ready-made thick caramel sauce (optional)
cocoa powder, to serve (optional)

Place the Oreo cookies in a zip-lock bag and bash with a rolling pin or, if you don't have one, a clean glass bottle, until you have crumbs. You may need to do this in batches. Empty the crumbs into a large mixing bowl, stir in the melted butter and peanut butter and mix well. Spoon the biscuit mix into a 23cm (9in) deep tart tin and press it into the base and up the sides. Chill the tin in the fridge for at least 1 hour.

Meanwhile, mix a tablespoon of cream with the cornflour in a bowl. Place the remaining double cream in a medium saucepan over a low heat. Once the cream is gently steaming, remove from the heat and whisk in the chocolate, cornflour paste and the butter. Whisk until smooth, stir in the milk and sprinkle in the salt, then allow to cool for about 20 minutes. Take the tart case from the fridge and scatter the chopped peanuts over the base. Spoon over the caramel sauce, if using. Pour the chocolate sauce over the nuts and caramel then smooth over. Place the tart in the fridge to chill and set for about 2 hours before serving. Dust with cocoa powder, if you like. This tart will last for about two days in the fridge.

INDEX

Managing Director: Sarah Lavelle
Project Editor: Sofie Shearman
Series Designer: Katy Everett
Designers: Katherine Case and Alicia House
Photography: Louise Hagger, Faith Mason, Alex Luck
Food Styling and Recipes: Lucy O'Reilly, Emily Kydd, Rosie Reynolds,
Pip Spence, Rebecca Woods, Sue Quinn
Prop Stylist: Alexander Breeze, Rachel Vere, Louise Hagger
Additional Text: Sofie Shearman
Head of Production: Stephen Lang
Senior Production Controller: Sabeena Atchia

Published in 2024 by Quadrille Publishing Ltd

Recipes extracted from *Posh Toast, Posh Eggs, Posh Kebabs, Posh Pancakes,
Posh Potatoes, Posh Rice, Posh Sandwiches* and *Posh Pasta*.

Quadrille Publishing Ltd
52-54 Southwark Street
London SE1 1UN
www.quadrille.com

Cataloguing in Publication Data: a catalogue record for this book is
available from the British Library.

Text © Quadrille Publishing Ltd 2024
Photography © Louise Hagger, Faith Mason and Alex Luck 2015-2020
Design and layout © Quadrille 2024

ISBN: 978 1 83783 2 491

Printed in China

MIX
Paper | Supporting
responsible forestry
FSC™ C020056